before grapes become wine

BOOK ONE

MOON ABOVE MY WORLD

a novel way with poetry

Alan C. Fleming

All rights reserved. Except as permitted, no part of this publication may be reproduced, distributed or transmitted in any form or by any means, or stored in a database or retrieval system, without the prior written permission of the publisher.

This work is fiction. Names and characters, places and incidents are either the product of the author's imagination or are used fictitiously. Any resemblance to actual persons, living or dead is entirely coincidental.

Find Alan C. Fleming on Twitter: @alancfleming

E-mail address: alanfleming168@gmail.com

ISBN (Paperback) 978-0-9949312-0-7
ISBN (eBook) 978-0-9949312-1-4

Copyright @2016 by Alan C. Fleming
All rights Reserved
First Edition – March 2016

"Sometimes a season is as short as we make it or as long as we dream it possible."

Alan C. Fleming

DEDICATION

Buen Camino

This book is dedicated to **Operators of Albergues**
located along the way of
Camino de Santiago de Compostela.

Words alone cannot express sufficient gratitude, operators, staff and volunteers deserve for their efforts in providing safe shelter, heaven's best Pilgrim hospitality and much needed comfort for a good night's sleep. Operators of *Albergues* deserve everlasting recognition as being the biggest contributor to the magic of individual journey. More than smiles, I feel love for the greatness each *Albergue* provides in keeping journey moving forward.

Este libro esta dedicado a todos los operadores de los albergues ubicados a lo largo del camino de Santiago de Compostela. No hay palabras que puedan expresar la gratitud y el reconocimiento que merecen los operadores y voluntarios de los albergues por sus esfuerzos para proveer hospitalidad y confort al cansado peregrino necesitado de la ansiada noche de descanso después del largo trayecto del diario caminar. Ellos son unos de los principales contribuyentes en hacer del Camino algo mágico para cada individuo. Amo, no solo sus sonrisas de bienvenida, sino también la maravillosa actitud de mantener la jornada orientada siempre hacia adelante.

"Buen Camino Peregrino"

Camino-Related Poems

2	Yellow Arrows	2
5	Inside Spiritual Journey	5
50	Dragonfly In Pilgrim Sight	54
60	Prince Pilgrim	65
65	Two Walking Sticks	71
74	Another Stone Has Stayed	80
80	I Am The Soul Beside Me	88
86	Spiritual Sounds Of The Camino	95
101	Third Time In Heaven	114
109	Dragonfly In Spain	122
115	A Million Steps Has Left A Saint	128
141	Spiritual Fracking	157

TABLE OF CONTENTS

	Introduction	iii
1	Beautiful Rainbows	1
2	Yellow Arrows	2
3	Streets Of Solidarity	3
4	Untie My Boat	4
5	Inside Spiritual Journey	5
6	Underneath An Olive Tree	6
7	Stalker	8
8	The Cocoon That Couldn't	9
9	The Violinist	10
10	An Orchard And A Garden	11
11	Draw A Picture	12
12	Summer Remembered	13
13	A Man Is Allowed To Cry	14
14	My Child Was Abducted	16
15	Apples Like Sheep	17
16	In Evergreen Forest	18
17	Galoshes My Inner Child Wears	19
18	Grand Fantasy	20
19	An Undelivered Kiss	22
20	The Wound That Never Heals	23

21	Private Collection	24
22	Red Roses Never Cut	25
23	Never Trust A Lover With A Sword	26
24	I Stepped Outside My Comfort Zone	27
25	Apple Orchard Frost	28
26	I Have Lyrics To Be Happy	29
27	Native Gorgeous - Virgin Ice	30
28	All Her Age Has Ripened	31
29	Ocean On Fire	32
30	Before This Season Leaves Me	33
31	Journey With A Rusted Heart	35
32	Magnificent Cathedral	36
33	Apple Trees In Autumn	37
34	The Last Petal On Her Daisy	38
35	I Have Been To The Next Season	39
36	Deaf Woman	40
37	A Flower With A Reason	41
38	Overlooking The Sea In Me	42
39	Butterfly Dance	43
40	Impermeable	44
41	Climbing On Ice Before It Melts	45
42	Two Roses, Uncut, Undelivered	46
43	Your Energy Attracts Me	47

44	Don't Judge Me For Liking Pleasure	48
45	Winter's Nicer Frost	49
46	Ashes In My Garden	50
47	Beyond Ego's Intuition	51
48	A Place Where You And I Can Go	52
49	Multiculturalism	53
50	Dragonfly In Pilgrim Sight	54
51	Poet - Last One To Surrender	56
52	Catching Butterflies	57
53	In A Garden Full Of Love	58
54	All I Ever Needed	59
55	I'd Like A Different Author Please	60
56	In Heaven No One Wants To Float	61
57	I Made It Rain	62
58	Modern Day Poem	63
59	Strawberry Stains Around Her Lips	64
60	Prince Pilgrim	65
61	Reincarnation	67
62	Let My Soul Return Me	68
63	Solitude Has No Shadow	69
64	Grace Of Acceptance	70
65	Two Walking Sticks	71
66	One Night Stand	72

67	I Found A Forest In My Dreams	73
68	Reconciliation	74
69	Soft Romance	75
70	Two Vineyards In My Smile	76
71	Silent Echoes	77
72	Moon Above My World	78
73	Would You Save Me If You Could?	79
74	Another Stone Has Stayed	80
75	Ballet Butterfly (Her Passion Dies)	81
76	I Used My Flashlight	83
77	Never Miss The Time It Takes	84
78	A Kiss Stealing Whispers	86
79	I Don't Need You To Love Me	87
80	I Am The Soul Beside Me	88
81	Poetry The Poem	89
82	Candy Floss	90
83	Popsicle love	91
84	Dark Love Unlike Chocolate	92
85	Sandcastles To Return To	94
86	Spiritual Sounds Of The Camino	95
87	Like A Rainbow Never Knowing Storm	97
88	To Where Once We Were	98
89	Inside Oceans	99

90	Flash Mob Hugging	100
91	Terracotta Soldier	101
92	Sparkles In My Eyes	102
93	At Ripened Age	103
94	I Will Love Her with My Body	104
95	In Winter Standing	105
96	Magnificent Failure	106
97	Age Of White	107
98	Bridge Over Bipolar Waters	110
99	Removing Water From Your Ego	111
100	On Untold Edge	112
101	Third Time In Heaven	114
102	Retrieving Heart	115
103	Moments With Amore	116
104	Rainbows Now In Braille	117
105	Heart In Free Fall	118
106	I'll Let My Echo Stay	119
107	Second Heart	120
108	Spent Memories	121
109	Dragonfly In Spain	122
110	Arctic Bouquet	123
111	One Of Me Is Broken	124
112	Tears Become My Blood	125

113	My Heart Is In Her Storm	126
114	Abandoned Memory	127
115	A Million Steps Has Left A Saint	128
116	Spring Blossoms	129
117	Darling We Have Baggage	130
118	All Signs Say She's A Keeper	131
119	I Chased Her One Last Time	132
120	I Bled With A Heart That Would Not Die	133
121	She Stole My Only Copy	134
122	She Keeps Burning All Her Treasures	135
123	Before Nature Gave Me Feelings	136
124	When Peace Returns From War	137
125	Eight Minutes Of Descent	138
126	Inward Child Of My Pain	139
127	Let Love's Bridge To Drama Fall	140
128	Broken Promise	141
129	Zen Love	143
130	Inside My Soul, Emotions Save Me	144
131	Masturbation - Insane Lover For A Day	145
132	Silence Too Loud	146
133	Man Gets Old	147
134	Passageway To Autumn Soul	148
135	Beneath Stars Awaiting	149

136	You Became My Flag	150
137	Demeanor	151
138	Dhyana And Dark Chocolate	153
139	Halfway Point Between Two Consenting Adults	155
140	I Am Not Too Cold To Cuddle	156
141	Spiritual Fracking	157
142	She Is Less Than Half My Age	160
143	Another Kiss Before I Die	161
144	My Inner Child Crying	162
Acknowledgements		163

PRAISE FOR

before grapes become wine
MOON ABOVE MY WORLD

Verse after verse, Alan invites us to join him on his joyous journey of self-discovery, a journey where he shares not only his joys, his pains and his love, but an emerging awareness of a self that had often remained hidden. Alan deals with feelings of aloneness and abandonment which are never far from life's real day to day adventures. Alan's poetry is a touching and engaging reminder of the human person that lives deep within us.
--Andre Bergevin, Canadian Writer.

Brilliance of simplicity.
Alan has a way with words persistent and playful with the subconscious mind. Alan C. Fleming has crafted Old School, New School and No School with near perfection. If anyone can inspire a Global Recovery of Poetry, he can.
--Barry Spilchuk - The Legacy Coach
Coauthor - A Cup of Chicken Soup for the Soul®
580 million copies sold.

Introduction

To understand peace, love and happiness one has to live for it.

September 2004 I walked the *Camino de Santiago de Compostela* for the first time. The Camino has since stayed within me. Like an apostle of the Camino, I often encourage others to do this Pilgrimage.

May 2010 I underwent open heart surgery. The procedure involved an aortic valve replacement. From that date forward, with heart repaired, my way of thinking changed significantly. My outlook towards everyday life became greatly altered. Life became unequivocally precious. I began to sense spiritual attunement with the universe. In 2012, I returned to the Camino. I returned again in 2014.

While walking The Camino, September 2012, I became inspired to write, to do more travelling and most importantly to stop and smell the roses. With a rusty heart from life's blisters and bruises, I began to realize just how important it is to be one's own best friend.

Much of my poetry happens in isolation as internal dialogue where both my heart and soul interact. It is from deep within at origin of tears where words emerge before leaping forward to become ways with poetry.

I enjoy writing as an exploration of perspectives. I believe energy forces never stop interacting within the psyche of a person. As poet I can play on both sides of perspective. As artist I am able to paint different scenarios using creative imagination. We are all carpenters of journey, each of us building stairways to next levels of understanding.

Sentiments become important factors when harvesting outlook. I stay with premise, happiness is found, not waited for.

We are each distinctly different, despite our souls have so much in common. My poetry explores a multitude of themes, including: heartbreak, closure, relationship, morality, physical aging, death, spirituality, sexuality, love and romance.

In Book One, MOON ABOVE MY WORLD, I incorporate personal tears of journey as background to deriving mindset. From there I narrate on a variety of themes. Read my poetry without prejudice. Read my poetry without focusing on the fiction of its creative content. Let yourself be victim to this sometimes rebellious way of thinking. Enable yourself the freedom to examine another perspective.

Book One also includes twelve poems relating to life's journey as inspired while walking the *Camino de Santiago de Compostela.*

Alan C Fleming

1

Beautiful Rainbows

You gave me beautiful rainbows.
You gave me many.
I am sorry if I gave you only storms.

You gave me hugs, you gave me kisses.
You gave me plenty.
I am sorry if I gave you only thorns.

You gave me happiness, you gave me joy.
Mostly you gave me hope.
I wish you would have given me tomorrow.

2

Yellow Arrows
(Camino de Santiago)

in solitude, the same.
every day is my Camino,
never abandoned
I keep finding yellow arrows.

never without burden
I carry origins of different sorrows,
each step releasing something from my past.
seasons changing, I keep moving forward.

prayers of acceptance embracing no regret.
I cross bridges.
I cross horizons never before visited,
yellow arrows guiding.

where everyone is sharing
one final destination.
every other pilgrim
in solitude, the same.

3

Streets Of Solidarity
(in honor of political prisoners in Venezuela)

Standing brave against fascist crime,
alive to rescue freedom.
With eyes that glittered
they stood their ground.

Saviors of democracy,
those who gave their lives.
Their souls kept strong within our hearts
to achieve a better life.

Dialogue was their only weapon.
Social media was their sword.
Never any mention of surrender
against a regime that kept on killing.

Against lies of education.
Standing proud their colleagues did.
Now young souls locked in prison,
advocates of right, denied true vision.

In prayers I shall remember
when freedom was at risk,
each one a hero of their time,
each one a hero of their time.

In prayers I shall remember.
In prayers I shall remember.

4

Untie My Boat

Lend me water.
Lend me bread.
I will pay you with a smile.

I'm a wealthy man.
I have a heart and soul.
I have visions, I have dreams.

I have empty pockets and a life to live.

Untie my boat.
There is a place for you.

I will share my water.
I will share my bread.
You can pay me with a smile.

5

Inside Spiritual Journey
(Camino de Santiago)

A cross was visible through early morning mist.
In penance, I surrendered all preoccupations.
The pain of yesterday's blisters momentarily forgotten.

Empty of hesitation, passageway to inward journey,
I found a part of me I had not yet known.
I cannot go home the same man I came.

Tears inside delicate sanctuary within quiet soul
altered during lifetime, my constitution now needs revising.
I allowed myself to cry. It took me deeper.

On pathway beneath quiet moon and star-filled dream
I journeyed through moments of reminiscing mind,
stepping beyond frown, recognizing blessed be divine,
each day another way.

Fear of not succeeding choired away by noiseless charm.
Childhood kites suspended in currents of wishful winds.
Little miracles embracing, gracing sweet sense of who I am;
jubilant I become, leaving both pain and stone behind.

Inside spiritual journey,
prayers I stay forever within this timeless space.
Beneath cotton-pillowed skies,
everyone an angel, in mid-life I feel divine.
If I have choice as some souls have stayed,
eternal in this way.

6

Underneath An Olive Tree

Sitting on a mountainside with full view of the sea,
sheltered by welcoming shade underneath an olive tree,
in a daze looking straight ahead with nothing on my mind,
I am here alone because my woman left me.

Reddish weathered pebbles scattered on hillside soil,
I imagine how refreshed they feel every time it rains.
Looking up I see a sky of un-ripened olives soon to go to market.
As far as my squinting eyes can see, I see ripples under midday sheen.

How many of my tears would it take to flood this mountain?
Silently thinking sadly to myself
or could the valley on the other side be flooded by my sadness?
In either case my woman left me.

Lucie the waitress wearing a bare back dress,
Yes the one who winked at me.
I never flirted with her. That is what my woman claims. She is wrong.
I have been as faithful as can be.

It's not nice being accused of things one does not do.
I could have smiled at the bartender.
Much prettier she is than the waitress, her gestures more inviting
With cleavage that keeps on selling beer.

I stayed faithful to my woman. Now I am on a hillside
with nothing on my mind, no one by my side.
Underneath an Olive Tree,
I am here alone because my woman left me.

The olive tree my witness, I have been here many times before.
My lady gets a little edgy. She fabricates each time accusing.
In a daze, looking straight ahead with nothing on my mind
I am here alone because my woman left me.

7

Stalker

Oceans divided upon frozen dream,
my bleeding heart never thawing.
Walk between my thoughts
I will be there always.

She left me before last chapter read,
significant to reoccurring love.
Conscience forever following,
distance my savior, silence my storm.

Stalker forever hiding in my heart
camouflaged as pending dream-come-true.
When thoughts resurface in my mind
I know forever she is near.

I wait for her inside first meeting place.
Two single espressos served on life's wobbly table.
I sit beside my past
reminiscing as if nothing ever happened.

Age now finds me unprepared.
Life has taken all of autumn's best.
Memories greying in my eyes,
all is gone except illusion love is real.

The Cocoon That Couldn't

When niceness has no butterfly
some cocoons just can't.
Metamorphosis stays unknown.
Caterpillar is all some have.

Some get tangled within self-made net
creating prison inside darkness.
Butterflies kept caged through summer season,
without a flutter, without good reason.

Never inward knowing, eyes stay outward shut.
Never transformation, no dancing in the skies,
everything else she wants is hers to have.
The purity of my love is mine to keep.

9

The Violinist

A child with miraculous talent,
off stage she is like gentle rainfall.

In performance
she becomes a journey through unbroken spirit.
I have no adult left inside me,
only audience
to admire sweet child prodigy.
Her destiny is a blessing
to ears deep within searching soul.

I become spring breeze,
dancing on weightless sky.
Dragonflies within my vision
in concert with childhood dream.
I am within myself.
I know where heaven is.

Sweet virgin
delicate in angelic white;
she is too innocent
to understand perfection.

Her violin mesmerizes me.
I surrender all my senses.

I close my eyes
to stay tranquil within my being.
In wild silence
I lose myself.

10

An Orchard And A Garden

In loneliness I keep believing
autumn fruit is most divine.
The cycle of life knows best.
The essence is of time.

In solitude I keep returning
to where I want to be.
With you it seems impossible.
Seasons they keep dying.

It is faith that keeps me waiting
for the night of the harvest moon.
Two apples side by side,
both clinging to one same branch.
You and I will forever be
refusing to fall,
stubbornly refusing to start again.

Our only orchard is what we in life create.
Our self-made garden is all that keeps our journey sweet.
One apple is insufficient when two stay wanting,

an orchard and a garden.

11

Draw A Picture

Draw a picture of the sun.
Hold it high above your head
to hide darkened skies that cloud your day.
Things will change, they always do.
Have patience dear.
Believe this too.

Draw a picture of a heart.
Hold it to the center of your chest
to hide broken dreams that lose their way.
Things will change, they always do.
Have patience dear.
Believe this too.

Draw a picture of who you think you are.
Hold it up beside what others draw of you.
Now compare differences of what perspectives say.
Things will change if you do too.
Have patience dear.
Believe this too.

12

Summer Remembered

Heart with impaired vision,
soul unsheltered in the cold.
Fabric of reconciliation
in whiteout to the winds.
Hope my only gesture,
visible as droplets in the air.
I prayed she would return
to soothe frozen dream.

I have no mitts for winter, only wishes.
I keep no scarf, no rescue in me.
I remember
cuddling with her inside summer hammock,
bathing in the warmth of happy smiles.
Now this day breathless
inside swirls of winter blizzard.
Summer memories gone.

I am here
between true love and another season.
Deeply sensitive to a place I'd rather never be.
Rust marks on my wrists.
Agony of countless days remaining.
I hear love in someone else's song.
Overtone to last words spoken
I remember summer.

13

A Man Is Allowed To Cry

A tree of butterflies is what I saw
when I emerged from a night long sleep.
I am at a crossroads. Change is on my mind.
I must escape this inward journey.
I seek a different place.

Overcome with tears,
weathered by torrential skies,
navigating through storms,
relentless efforts before I die.
Hearts don't shrink when they get wet,
a man is allowed to cry.

I need not know where you are coming from
nor must you know where I have been.
When life pinches it leaves a bruise
until we all start changing colors.

If you and I can forget cocoons,
metamorphosis
will leave our caterpillars in the past.
No more wars. The strategy is,
you and I must learn to fly.

We are flesh first before religions.
We are heart and soul
sharing one same vision.

Let us embrace one another
and in defiance of what we are told
we can or cannot do,
let us drink wine from one same goblet,
to honor our differences.
Let us be graced by rainbows
before raindrops turn to storms.

In pursuit of the country worth saving
is Peace on Earth.

14

My Child Was Abducted

There is no way back without my soul.
I am his mother. He is every mother's son.
No one there to help me,
my child is abducted.

Heaven help is where I want to be
somewhere beyond a river full of tears.
Starting with a little strength,
my castle it will find me.

Happy again is how I want to feel
when I fulfill my promise to return,
when I walk away from darkest cloud
to find my journey waiting.

There is no way back without my soul.
When tears are dry I will build profoundly,
an iron gate, a heart of gold.
It took away my heart to build.
My child was abducted.

15

Apples Like Sheep

apples like sheep

one after the other
under the allure of fall
orchards become naked
by winter's call

all wanting to cuddle
each believing in spring
with cold weather coming
frozen tempers will sing

refusing to fall
inspiring each other
two stayed on one branch
remembering summer

I was one who stayed clinging
I know the routine
the other my lover
we looked so pristine

we had to fight winters
to even scare crows
our sweetness we shared
with magic we glowed

it's not easy being different
every other one the same

apples like sheep

16

In Evergreen Forest

In evergreen forest,
mist upon my morning
like a quiet pastel painting,
tranquility seldom found.

Clarity disappearing.
Time remaining infinitely short.
When I am gone, I will not cry
nor will I let sadness have me.

Forgiveness no longer in my focus.
The last few moments
of journey, they are mine.
It's time for celebration.

My heart quietly weakens.
Without pulse, I shall be ready
to define this night eternal,
sweet horizons forever staying.

Pines will stand tall where I am seeded.
Memories will stay in eagle's nest.
My pride will fly each day high
in evergreen forest.

17

Galoshes My Inner Child Wears

Galoshes my inner child wears stay drenching wet,
my childhood not far behind me.
Memories unworthy have faded with disappearing time.

I caught tadpoles in the creek
behind where my childhood lived.
Moments stopped in journey,
few have survived this far by choice.
All things are few,
my treasure chest now nearly empty.
I let things go,
knowing I could not keep them.
In life we gather memories when we can.

Purity of innocence is where my wealth stays hidden.
Galoshes my inner child wears stay drenching wet,
my childhood not far behind me.

18

Grand Fantasy

Grand fantasy:
The music speaks to me.
Frederic Chopin - Grand Valse Brillante.

The concert is sold out.
I am content listening to the music.
Alone I have standing room only.

I look outside my window
to notice someone waltzing in my vision.
She is a gypsy and my piano her Irish lover.
My laugh becomes restless.
With sad overture I smile in concert.

I am returned to our first acquaintance,
coffee and clumsy conversation,
mindfulness of bliss, poetry in my smile.

The lady's delicate motion
whispers nothing.
Content without applause
she softly identifies with the waltz.

I see precious innocence,
sparkling in her eyes, unravelling into lust.
She leaves me puzzled.

Discontent with innocence,
she dances for freedom.
Her ambition cannot contain the freedom she is seeking.
She is overwhelmed by energy.
With unrelenting desire,
somewhere within her being, she is afraid
of love's commitment.

The music speaks to me.
Frederic Chopin
Grand Valse Brillante in E flat major Op. 18
Grand Fantasy

19

An Undelivered Kiss

There is never any oxygen
inside an undelivered kiss.
I cannot live without you.
All of you is what I miss.

You were my sunshine
when we met,
my entire world
wherever we would go.

When you drenched me with your storm,
I waited for a rainbow.
Now there is no more weather in your forecast,
no more calendar in your heart.

There is never any oxygen
inside an undelivered kiss.
I cannot live without you.
All of you is what I miss.

20

The Wound That Never Heals

If you cannot find reason to be with me,
be the memory in my dream.

If you cannot find season to love me,
be the lyrics in my song.

In this lifetime if you choose to live without me,
be my wound that never heals.

21

Private Collection

Find happiness
amongst pebbles and stones
when you cannot have the mountain.
You must not squint
or you will not find them.
Keep collecting. Do not possess them.
Just keep collecting.
They come as recollections.
Once you have them,
add them to your private collection.

Red Roses Never Cut

Should you ever have a change of heart,
I am where last you always left me.
Beautiful dreams may not come easy.
Let's relive everlasting from the start.

Our garden was only half in bloom.
Red roses never cut.
Dark clouds were never in the plan.
I am ready dear. I know we can.

Love can hurt much more than we desire.
The sun will rise each time we let it set.
Let hearts forever keep embracing.
Let eternity stay ours to forever keep.

Reconciliation can take forever.
I pray forever it may take.
Uncut roses will one day bloom.
Bouquet pending, together soon.

23

Never Trust A Lover With A Sword

Never trust a lover with a sword.
Be gone instead with a broken heart.
When yesterday keeps hurting,
let that be the bridge you cross.

My heart grows deep.
Earth around my root.
Bipolar like tsunami.
She threw it all away.

Journey takes me further,
by sunrise another dream.
Another day will bless me,
heartwarming if I try.
This love inside me needs to die.

Alone my heart must find its way.
The love I have grows strong within,
is who I am, not she.
Another love when romance dies.
A second heart will save me.

24

I Stepped Outside My Comfort Zone

I stepped outside my comfort zone.
Confidence crossed over with me.
Everything appeared much the same
except old fears I did away with.

It's time I leave my cast in stone.
It's time I find my true way home.
I will not bathe in yesterday's grief.
God Bless I settle, not with new ones.

I stepped outside my comfort zone.
Confidence crossed over with me.
It's time I leave my cast in stone.
It's time I find my true way home.

25

Apple Orchard Frost

I see winter frozen on naked branch
two apples dangling from a season past
apple orchard frost without mention of renewal
warmth of spring breeze abandoned
magic of summer forgotten

I see love growing inside wounded heart
without morning dew to grace it
spring fever finding sanctuary inside hopeless dream
butterflies frozen in lethargic sky
solitude captive to faded quarrel

aging as an apple does once touched by frost
I see inner sweetness wrinkled by winds that sour season
am I a heartbreak from the past
or a memory waiting for a song
with visions weary I hold my journey nearer

26

I Have Lyrics To Be Happy

Feeling inclusive
amongst smiles of equal value.
Let me share my jubilance with you.
Butterfly skies high above your garden.

This day is perfect for a song.
I have lyrics to be happy.
You and I,
finding magic in the air.

My forest is the air above your flower.
I'll do just what I can
to keep all your seasons friendly.
Journey proud to let things be,
every smile together fine.

This day is perfect for a song.
I have lyrics to be happy.
You and I, finding magic in the air,
never again inside darkness.
Let us stay up in the sky.

27

Native Gorgeous - Virgin Ice

sugar coated rose
love can have me if it wants me

love medicine
smother me with affection
hooked on devastation
please remove me from my pain
I feel wanted when you kiss me

native gorgeous
nature's finest
broken seasons left behind
pierce me gently with your arrow
I have buffalo hair where others keep their tiger

virgin ice
my eyes I keep inside you
polar bears inside my veins
I feel abandoned when you leave me
in your arms
the only place where I can stay
if you accept the current of my river
I will please you
before ice clots lose their water

history put darkness in my skies
there is more to me than surface
I have history in my color
race is in my land.
I am here forever darling
give me status when you can

28

All Her Age Has Ripened

With prudish mind,
she exposes autumn bloom.
Petals purely white
much like goat milk.
Garden's favorite rose,
sweet like cotton candy.
Chagall would love her too.
Happier than lilies of the valley,
enough she inspires
Japanese to use their cameras

Virgin of a last remaining season
still awaiting harvest.
Everything more delicious
without reference to the past.
All her age has ripened.
Memories golden, hidden treasure.
Come and have me, echoes in her whisper.
Every kiss, uncontrollably aging.
Somewhere within this woman
I find her lady waiting.

Girlish charm
worth twice her weight in friendly kiss.
When time begins to wrinkle
I put it there to touch her heart.
Spellbound I get inside her.
With gestures spilling from my skin,
desire deeper than with words,
my thoughts are mixed with dizzy.
Prudish story keeps me staying.
Sweet silence overcomes me.

29

Ocean On Fire

Sunset will teach you
why you must let some things go.
It's the only way to get there.
Passageway to another day,
where freely a heart can grow.

Be not the owner
of another person's world.
Fabricate no law to hold them.
When moments in time
have come and gone,
let sunset burn your ocean.

This will free you from attachment.
Through matters known to your soul
your bridge will take you
to another place you will want to be.
When you awaken,
another day will greet you
where freely a heart can grow.

30

Before This Season Leaves Me
(Beneath Strawberry Moon)

Gentle rains caressing blissful imaginations,
two seagulls chirping as they watched us kiss.
Energies found only in nature,
celebrating where feelings extinguish fire.
Rainbows teasing
under signature of a strawberry moon.

Soul soothing water beneath a changing sky,
she kept me mesmerized
by the intensity of her lady.
Rhapsody of banquet
so delicious I kept thinking selfishly to myself.
Could a moment be so rejuvenating
when all my wounds still hurting?

Unguarded boundaries,
tangos dancing on hungry tongues.
We stopped time
for as long as it took to engage the moment.
Devoured internally by escaping thoughts,
rebellious to my morals.
Sometimes it rains.
Sometimes minds get drenched in bliss.

Rainbows bridging overcast
from dark and distant storms.
Presence of surrender
breaking through overhanging skies.
At the precise moment
when my fingers touched her treasure,

I sensed friendship would have limited time
before finding closure.

Toiling for pleasure she and I had different reasons,
never longevity on our minds.
In my arms I would hold her
for as long as the moment shares.
Teach me not to hold passion as possession
but to eat the fruit of a harvest season.
I want to be prepared in mind
and well harvested before this season leaves me.

31

Journey With A Rusted Heart

Memories are things that tarnish.
The hurting ones
never stop rusting the heart.

Unless your sense of forgiveness
awakens sooner
when every time it dies,
evidence is all that's needed
sufficient to bid farewell
for the fifteen hundredth time.

The beds we broke
will one day be repaired.
All tears will one day dry.
Nothing more will ever hurt
except journey
with a rusted heart.

The beds we broke
will one day be repaired.
All tears will one day dry.
Nothing more will ever hurt
except journey
with a rusted heart.

32

Magnificent Cathedral

Inside my person
a magnificent cathedral stands.
Its doors are always opened.
Come inside it tells each soul
whenever your heart desires.
My spirit echoes this aloud
to anyone who listens.

First I invite the beggar.
Then I invite the thief.
I invite the politician who defies all rules.
I invite the ISIS terrorist too.
Everyone down on your knees,
this lesson is for you.
Religion is just an institution.

There is no need to let morality die,
nor any reason
to prove your mother wrong.
You were born in this world to be my brother,
you and I, same energies in our smiles.
Should you be one to kill me,
your morality would be first to die.

Next I invite the hypocrite,
I invite the preacher too.
I invite all people of false pretense.
Give me died and gone to heaven.
Everyone down on your knees,
This lesson is for you:
Religion is just an institution.

33

Apple Trees In Autumn

Reminiscing
beyond sweet summer breeze.
Well spent seasons,
now a part of who I am.

Selective memories staying with me,
some things are not forgotten.
Warmth of autumn harvest
not far from winter frost.

Orchards of my youth
now seen with clouded eyes.
Apple trees in autumn.
Can I be your friend forever?

I know when apple blossoms bloom.
If you will keep me on your branch,
I promise I will not leave you.
All my dreams now ripened.

When I close my eyes
an image of an apple stays.
Orchards forever inside apple pie
if another soul will have me.

34

The Last Petal On Her Daisy

Waiting for things to get better, wisdom lies.
Mankind has tested this theory many times before
to little or no avail. It is up to inward journey
to fix pathways going forward.

Painstakingly, everything has been tried before.
The last petal on her daisy should never be dismissed.
It is up to inward journey to awaken heart before it dies,
to take risk to leave one world before entering yet another.

Purgatory if you fail to try.
Heartbreak will engrave itself inside ego's stubborn mind.
Foolish are those who leave heart behind.
Beleaguered becomes a wounded soul when never having tried.

Fear is least of all your friends.
It can rob you of heart's content.
It can leave you nowhere else to go.
Awaken to your powers, look inward for the answers.

35

I Have Been To The Next Season

I have been to the next season a hundred times before.
A raindrop thought itself wise, pitter-pattering to a dandelion.
Better to accept where autumn winds are blowing
when fluff is all you have.
An early rain may not come late.
Your journey much decides your fate.

There are cycles in life
from beneath a blanket of snow so deep.
Reawaken in spring from darkest sleep.
Your dandelion will look the same again
as many fields before you keep.
It's the politics of nature being played again.

Be wise, be learned, nature will repeat itself.
No need to fear seasons in advance.
Your only lesson in this life to learn,
to dance beneath quiet clouds of passing skies,
to drink from wines at harvest time, and
to use your seeds to be dandelion again.

36

Deaf Woman

She was the only girl I knew
who remained silent
when bread tasted stale.
Ironically she would never shut up.
So many gestures she had to share.

Her screams during orgasm
I could hear them through her eyes.
Accented with French kisses,
enough to make any woman sigh.
So loud she could each time she tried.

With pencil she used outspoken words
yet every compliment went unheard.
Boisterous spirit dancing like silent dove,
noiseless soulmate awakening eternal love.
She was without a doubt,
unsilenced in my heart as no other person could.

37

A Flower With A Reason

In one day my garden grew, a little.
In less than one full season
my flowers bloomed.

No storm can deprive
a flower from desire
when it wants full bloom.

I was fine until the gardener cut me.
Goodness I still have
doing what I can.

I give fragrance. I give spirit
to sentiments that need uplifting
anywhere life lets me.

Emotions make me wet all over
beneath people's valid tears,
some in mourning, others in their smiles.

A yellow flower tells an empty heart
words it wants to hear. Evidence of love
can never completely vanish.

I see myself not as victim but as promise
in journey doing goodness,
a flower with a reason.

38

Overlooking The Sea In Me

Quaint coastal villages take me there
on a scooter climbing cliffs, mountainside edges,
overlooking the sea in me.

In perfect balance I stop in the shade
of an olive tree. Heaven prey I find sweet grapes.
Orchards of imagination give me fruit, my soul
the warmth required, to be in heaven for a day.

Consume me whispers echoes in the air.
Sweet songs of seashores caress sparkles in my eyes.
Not standing on my feet, cloud nine beside me
on a scooter by the sea.

Listening to ancient winds, sanctuary inside seashells,
in heaven I become the sea. Not craving to possess,
solemnly without attachment, peace becomes my smile.

A scooter took me there, so did sweet desire.
Ripples foreplay serenity in my eyes.
With heaven visited, I cannot die.

I dream sweet kisses become a bridge. I am joined
with my other shore. When I return from deep within
I find myself inside yet another dream.

Plenty of jubilance in my heart.
Between unsheltered emotions, I share
my shadow with myself, overlooking the sea in me.

39

Butterfly Dance

Butterfly dance unseen by caterpillar.
All that matters is redefining journey.

Along the way, caterpillar came across a frog,
Can you identify with darkness?
caterpillar asked the frog.

Looking at the caterpillar,
We all need night, frog replied.
There are days when caterpillars need to sleep.

Inside journey,
caterpillar wormed another question to the frog.
What do you think of butterflies?

Beautiful things that fly. They put color in my sky.
croaked the frog.

Caterpillars inside cocoons - do they qualify?
The frog then sighed, I am happy being me.
I defend all rights to let caterpillars sleep.
Quirky frog did not miss a chance.
This world needs more color,
less caterpillars with double face.
I cannot tell which end is their behind.

Awakened to a dream, a butterfly emerged
wanting to teach frog to fly.
All the frog could do was dance.

Butterfly, in the steps that followed,
flew away.

40

Impermeable

I have seen sheep.
I made it half way through love
before getting hurt.
My morals became locked inside escaping prayer.

She was impermeable with no gentleness of mind remaining
like a cheated wife who screws with other people's heads.
I believed in romance.
She believed in promises pending.

Time gaps stole my sanity.
Her storm produced no rainbow.
I let her go.
I watched her leave.

Life kept me living on the edge of beyond reasonable doubt.
She kept me one juror away from verdict.
Getting wounded is an unnecessary distraction;
Blood stained heart, a giveaway.

Storyline had one page missing.
Before it was over
I had a relapse,
twice heartbroken by the same woman.

41

Climbing On Ice Before It Melts

Like climbing on ice before it melts,
her state of innocence will not be there
once warmth of life has touched her.

Purity surrenders before committing sin.
I can no longer think of her with innocent mind,
every part of me wants inside.

If I get lost before heaven finds me,
I may not wish to be born again.
This state of ecstasy should never end.

I never want to go alone.
When I go there, I will go there with my soul.
I will take my heart for heaven's binge.

Her beauty never ages inside dream.
My man grows old before pulse surrenders.
I am not selfish but a passing season.

Two Roses, Uncut, Undelivered

Two roses, uncut, undelivered
both coming from under nourished gardens
nestled between dandelions on opposite sides of earth.

In blissful passion each rub their buds
releasing milky sap into pretentious minds.
Neither having heart to give full bloom.

Beleaguered to horrendous storms
their pricks get in the way.
Gardens become devastated.
Flowers of reconciliation abandoned.

Lady rose reclaims her broken rainbow.
Two steps backwards she returns to soul
to a garden without soil.
With tears from ego she survives.

Imaginations enrage, each denying a love they both desire.
Letting tomorrow be lost to broken hearted promise,
neither will know the world where this day belongs.
Everything is real that never happened.

Poet rose halfway across his broken bridge,
he thorns the memories that sought their bloom.
Overly sensitive to beckoning words,
to moving forward he defines unworthy.

Long distance cannot fix each other's hurting mind.
Sanctuary to unwanted reasons, inflictions continue deep.
Never knowing where to settle,
everything is real that never happened.

43

Your Energy Attracts Me

Absurd it is when we feel attached.
Is this a sign of weakness?
Born to be free, possessed by attachment,
your energy attracts me in mysterious ways.

Under conditions that life imposes,
staying in love is a lifetime task.
In solitude I sacrifice my every day.
Your energy attracts me in mysterious ways.

My heart each time, it bleeds for you.
When you are in time-gaps far away, all I ever do is hurt.
Missing you becomes my daily bread.
Your energy attracts me in mysterious ways.

Understand me please. I am here for a reason.
I lost my way. I need a friend.

Nihilist ad infinitum. I am here for a reason.
Reductio ad absurdum. I need a friend.

Love is much more than a bridge that joins two shores.
It can overcast a river where lovers drown.
Love is where death is born and freedom dies.

I am here for a reason. I need a friend.

44

Don't Judge Me For Liking Pleasure

I shall remember sweet heavens on my way to hell.
Don't judge me for liking pleasure.
It all starts with pulse inside my heart
and finishes with exuberance of happy soul.

Life's journey makes wine taste sweeter.
Every moment when I'm inside you,
the rest of my body understands
why I let morals take me deeper.

Your touch does magic to my mind.
I get shivers when I stand.
There is no sunrise more delicious,
no here-on-earth more warming.

You harbor innocence inside girlish charm
awaiting next stage of summer.
I cannot explain why it feels so good.
In the act of loving, we both grow wiser.

Fresh virgin spirit dressed in naked rain
preparing to drench sweet blossom.
All intense I hold my breath.
I reminisce with memories in the making.

Don't judge me for liking pleasure.

45

Winter's Nicer Frost

Gleaming winter frozen on forest naked branch,
Arctic thaw so far from truth.
Childhood blossoms become faded memories.
Without my scarf I cannot breathe.

My blood thickens by more than worldly news.
On my way to winter, I vaguely remember spring.
Come quickly my dear friend.
You will stay this time beside me.

Solitude beneath winter blanket where everything is pure,
mud on my galoshes now distant from the truth.
Little cleansing clouds in greying words I speak.
Winter's nicer frost, my friend I now do seek.

Autumn becomes lethargic under temperature of changing sun.
I knew you would come home to sort things through.
Winter dearest I have traveled far without you.
It gives me joy to rest in peace, this time with you.

46

Ashes In My Garden

When I refused to shake the devil's hand,
ice formed around the devil's eyes.
His hand turned cold.
That is what the next hand told me.
Destitute to devil's grin
I now do penance for a madman.

In the early morning of perpetual smile
my sun keeps rising on heaven's side.
To my delight I am always there to greet it.
Beneath clear blue skies,
destiny has me staying
through everlasting time.

I now survive as ashes in his garden,
basking in the sunshine of daylight dream
where devil's fire no longer matters,
where rains can only nurture.
My blooms are what I make them.
Pure goodness all I can.

47

Beyond Ego's Intuition

Sometimes my mind goes well beyond
where I cannot go,
letting light in when I least expect it.
I am not someone else,
probably because of fears I carry.
I spend my entire lifetime
evaluating everything that matters.

I wear yesterday's shoes. I get there fine,
going places
I should have left behind.
When it hurts
I come home to visit all things present
only to realize
every door stays shut behind me.

Why does darkness keep interrupting light
becomes my pathway forward.
I never wait for answers.
I let instinct take me
well beyond ego's intuition.
As I depart the fool, I begin to know

I can get there fine.

48

A Place Where You And I Can Go

Beyond hanging branches
I found my field.
In it was a vineyard.
My heart it was consumed.
There I dream to one day know
a place where you and I can go.

In searching for:

I went far beyond where hearts stay broken,
even further than where souls do flee.
I left behind screams once heard.

I emptied out my bucket list.
No more waiting while times unfold.
No more crying over things untold.

When I got closer I became aware
of such a place where I could feel most free.
No more expectations. Nothing painful to my heart.

No more compromises in my mind,
No more disappointments of any kind,
Love permitting, you can go there too.

49

Multiculturalism

fish beneath my city
away from *water*
unfamiliar to my ways
I will not judge you

moon above my world
high up in the *air*
whichever way I look
I accept the way you are

earth around my root
I once thought
you would not give me space
I grew within your ground

elements of imagination
inside loving *mind*
extinguishing *fire*
to make all things fine

multiculturalism
everyone together

50

Dragonfly In Pilgrim Sight
(Camino de Santiago)

Dragonfly in pilgrim sight,
it's not a dream if you don't come down.

On the Camino I found my heaven.
Sunrise staying in my heart, undisturbed by rain.
Inward journey nurturing garden soul.
Rediscovering fantasy with childhood vision.
Sweet innocence expanding 500 miles.
This is where I started journey.

Dragonfly in pilgrim sight,
spirituality, first time in flight.

Jubilance contained when reaching Santiago.
Embracing sadness unsure that I was finished.
Boots well worn, achievements strong.
Joyous were my tears, not having time to dry.
Ambushed by a million hugs.
Prayers this way would never end.

Dragonfly in pilgrim sight,
euphoria, I can fly.

It felt like I was floating amidst holy air.
Blisters of journey no longer hurting.
Returning to where before I came, unwilling.
Every smile engraved in rock solid dream.
Camino finding sanctuary, engaging self-esteem.
This, the place where I shall stay.

Dragonfly in pilgrim sight,
never losing promise to make things right.

Solitude blessed inside friendly space.
Every hug shared with Pilgrim grace.
Goodwill of others becomes everlasting song.
Acquainting with miracles never before strong.
Everyone smiling on everyone's dream.
Gloriously accepting, my way had just begun.

Dragonfly in pilgrim sight,
in this sky, where I shall stay.

51

Poet - Last One To Surrender

before love lost its fight
before reasons left me
I found my poet
whispering
inside aging soul

I escaped first time
unscathed by emotions dying
so did my creative mind

I kept truth caged inside purgatory
delaying heartbreak
until all of me was numb

politics of love
why does it have two faces

so many people sea-shelled
on lover's shore
time leaves each one empty

once brave to change this world
youth engaged before young heart losing faith
second heart weathered by deception
inner poet
last one to surrender

52

Catching Butterflies

Catching butterflies (of course)
to use for poetry.
(I've seen this before).

Or could they be
fisherman nets
getting tangled
in knots of toil?

The world
just wants me
to see everything the same.
If I must believe
what everyone is saying,
vigorously I will resist.

I know there is another way
against the politics of education.
Let me first use soap.

I want love. They want war.
I save flowers. They pull roots.

Treat me like I matter.
Accept this other way of thinking.
I will show you
where virtue exists for peace.

53

In A Garden Full Of Love

In a garden full of love
she claims
her flowers will not grow.
She is a gardener nurturing empty harvest.
Her flowers will not bloom
unless she changes water.

I have no right
to define her faults. Awaiting bloom,
mine are undernourished too.
I spend my time seeking inner light
with nowhere else to go.
All the flowers in my garden,
neither do they grow.

I am tired. I feel abandoned.
Inward journey is where I seek my truth.
I escape this place to live within
the only world I can.
Same advice I have for her.
Create an imaginary world.
The blooms you seek belong to you.
Leave one garden for another.

54

All I Ever Needed

Every day I find myself
changing,
everyday defining
for better or for worse.

All I ever needed was a better heart
to have loved her
well beyond
every rage she ever gave me.

All I ever needed was endurance
and perhaps
a deafened ear to listen.

All I ever needed was patience
and no more tongue to speak.
By speaking I brought demise.

All I ever needed was forgiveness
repeatedly
from the start.

If only
I could have needed less.

55

I'd Like A Different Author Please

Rages of uncontrollable anger
like thunder in my skies,
she keeps coming back to tell me,
she doesn't love me anymore.

She keeps me in suspense.
She has me always wondering
if the ending will ever change.
I'd like a different author please.

Perfectly selected words.
Forgiveness is written in different ways.
There is a nicer way to keep this story going,
another way to read me.

She claims bad words are mine.
She sees from one perspective only.
There is a nicer way to keep this story going,
another way to read me.

56

In Heaven No One Wants To Float

I could stay forever
with her lips upon my smile.
Precisely how I felt
yesterday,
every thought complacent
to every desire alive.

Today she is
a rainbow washed away,
unstoppable,
no more paradise in my sky.

In heaven
no one wants to float.
Touch her when she wants you.
Leave her when she's gone.

57

I Made It Rain

I
found myself
looking for the red one
in a tulip bed amongst mostly yellows.
Few of them were white.
Love
should never end this way.
You
were looking too.
I was looking for the red one,
seeking sunset.
Forever
believing it would bring tomorrow,
earlier if I hurried.
And,
from my perspective
this day had given me enough.
Forever
I only wanted red
when carelessly I stepped
on yellow. To white it did not matter.
In the process I crushed a lady bug.
No idea how this happened.
Now my shoes stay stained forever.
Forgive me.
It happened for a reason.
This day was marred with imperfection.
Then, without intention
I made it rain
by stepping on a spider.

58

Modern Day Poem

1. I #sex with #text . I see with #twitter.
2. I #speak dangerously while losing all my #freedom.
3. My #government keeps legislating **#~~HumanRights~~** WaysofGettingShot.
4. I #cry with #tears. My #tears are #real yet no one ever #listens.
5. #Help me whichever #God is willing.

59

Strawberry Stains Around Her Lips

Ottawa's two-lip festival should be banned.
it's too orgy for my garden, every bloom seductive.
Yet strawberries are just fine.
Some temptations do not touch me.

Happy smiles stay forever.
Sundrenched memories here to stay,
my age of childhood ripening.
Now when I see strawberries,
happy thoughts consume me.

When I was five, picking strawberries with my dad
his technique, the sweetest of them all.
Keep sunshine in you heart,
three in the basket, one disappearing in your smile.

Strawberry stains around my lips,
I always wondered if the farmer knew.
I was not stealing,
Birds would have eaten just as many.

Three grades later, strawberries with a girl from school.
Strawberries in her mouth, she could not say a thing,
neither when I kissed her.
Boyhood stains around her lips.
Two-lip festival had come of age.

60

Prince Pilgrim
(Camino de Santiago)

I cannot wait to re-visit my humble self,
too many favorite places where I have been.
Jubilant to hear all good things with tears,
overcoming obstacles,
letting go of fears,
is why I keep returning.

I rise before the sun to touch the morning of another.
Inward journey becomes my pathway going forward,
loving soul my harvest.
I am the way - you and I - Prince Pilgrim is my name.
The trail goes further,
heaven-on-earth acquainting.

Blistering achievements,
smiles rescuing uncollected memories.
Shades of Santiago forever staying,
sharing spaces, people's faces,
through eyes my window,
mankind beside me.

Forgiving cathedrals bearing sin,
rediscovering sanctuary,
spirituality awakening within joyous soul.
Soothing it is. Freedom inside journey.
Love's energy building.
Heaven in me.

Yellow arrows invite me further.
Destinations find another chamber in my heart.
Intervals greet me with 'Buen Camino' gestures.
In the morning I will say good bye.
It doesn't matter if we never meet again,
our souls will keep remembering.

61

Reincarnation

Each of them,
one brave soldier,
peacefully meditating
in the afterlife?

I looked inward
when seeing
a field of poppies.

They stood tall
resilient to the wind
preparing to embrace
whatever next day
would give them.

No fear of dying,
immortal gift
to next generation,
each allowing red
to be their color.

62

Let My Soul Return Me

Full moon reflecting on a thousand dragonflies
robbing darkness from my sky.
Thoughts within my soul enlightened.

No more tears to carry.
Rescue me from my sadness.
Mistakes can be forgotten.

Un-crowd me from tomorrow.
Love is pure without possession.
This broken bridge can carry one.

I want no distractions when my heart awakens,
when I cross this bridge to another shore.
Let love be mine. Let soul return me.

63

Solitude Has No Shadow

complacency
and the time it takes to think
can consume a lifetime

once gone
spirit may not come back

solitude has no shadow
only tears
distant from the truth

it doesn't matter if you have
only one flower in your garden.
you have earth
beneath sun
your sanctuary

let wisdom nurture
all that you desire
let one flower be your garden

64

Grace Of Acceptance

Strolling through a field of oats
before harvest steals my dream.
Together with my inner child
before this season leaves me.

Peace and tranquility
I have inside my spirit.
It's so nice to be within oneself
befriending with a smile.

Inclusive with my inner being,
I am happy on the inside.
Grace of acceptance,
embracing who I am.

The universe my blessing.
When I get older
I won't be needing memories,
I'll be busy making new ones.

65

Two Walking Sticks
(Camino de Santiago)

Two walking sticks,
they do not match. I have the same.
As well, I feel your pain,
unbearably trying to stop you.

Rest your mind every step you can,
your body, not far behind.
Blisters in your heart are healing,
your soul in spirit with you.

Today I have a Pilgrim's prayer.
I will carry it all day for you
and within each step
a healing cross to share.

When we get to where everyone is going
with laughter each can cry,
this time not from painful journey
this time, for love and glory.

66

One Night Stand

Lips not leaving space for words
heartbreak pursuing pleasure
I knew there was another kiss awaiting
next one would make things right

romance trying to escape
solitude of pain clenched in hurried love
I kept picking all her petals
anxiously awaiting outcome

she caressed me back to life
each time I became a different man
passageway to where bliss would have me stay
enjoying smiles through the night

sweet morning had no dew
one night stand is all she gave me

67

I Found A Forest In My Dreams

I found a forest in my dreams.
I had been there as a child.
I hunted rabbits there in winter.
I counted robins in the spring.

Since then, city planners transformed my forest
into rows and rows of asphalt lines
with iron lamps adorning vinyl sided dwellings.
Childhood aesthetics all destroyed;
no more dragonflies to dream.

Today I see an entrance
to an unfinished city-promised pathway
with a well-constructed do-not-enter sign,
neon lights exposing future site of something else
and beautiful landscape pending.

It's good I lived my childhood
way back when I did.
I may not have had same chance to dream.
To a city planner it doesn't matter.

With every new development
another forest gone. As child, each time
returning home, never without a smile.
A part of childhood innocence is now each day gone,
a part of me now non-existent.

68

Reconciliation

Some things are destined never to be heard.
Things I say use quiet words.
They become loud only when you listen.

I spend my journey collecting treasures.
I keep them secure inside my heart.
All of them I miss profoundly, never with possession.

I see myself in childhood, one of them is hungry.
Half my plate is empty, I share without a question.

Alone each time I seek reconciliation with my youth.
One of me is broken. I search inside to fix it.

My perspectives are forever changing. Who says
my ideologies are wrong? You see me as a rebel.
I see things the only way I can.

My soul defines me. Everything I see
reassures me who I am. Things you see belong to you.
I live each day inside my journey, profoundly
never with possession.

69

Soft Romance

She always wanted closure.
By virtue of forgiveness,
forever she keeps returning.
I will keep her in my mind
until my heart forgets her name.
Love's history needs forgetting.
Forever she is mine.

She stays forever.
I keep trying to forget her name.
Repeatedly I keep failing
in all attempts to leave her.
Nothing changes the way I feel.
Smiles she seldom gave me
are treasures I keep seeking.

Her love will never let me go.
Through romance
I keep trying to forget her name.
Each time when I am with her
in the arms of yet another,
my heart starts bleeding.
Forever she is mine.

70

Two Vineyards In My Smile

Along a rural side road, parked in shade away from scorching sun,
my knees firmly pressed on gravel's cutting edge,
my face darkened inside female shadow,
in full view of vineyard celebration, I kissed my woman's pleasure.

Passenger door wide open, it was a perfect day for love.
My lady sideways on her seat, skirt beneath first festival.
With unwavering determination
I shared my gestures with her smile.
In drenching echo, I knew she would surrender.

Inside lady vineyard, sweet harvest on my tongue,
Looking upwards to her eyes
I could taste sparkles in her wine.
Blissful appetite got quenched; afterwards, around the bend,
appetite got quenched again with sweet BBQ and wine.

A cheering crowd dressed in Sunday best. A western band
performing country fest, everyone enjoying autumn festival.
Everyone celebrating inside their vineyard, town not knowing
I had just been inside mine.

I did well to steal the moment. I did well to taste the wines.
Everyone in the crowd applauded.
On my face a sweet smile did reveal,
I had more than sweetness on my tongue,
I had two vineyards in my smile.

71

Silent Echoes

There is a silent echo in the air.
Its source is from within.
Like a Cathedral bell it never fails.
The message stays unchanged.
"I AM"

There are days when without it I would have no faith.
Meaningful this message is to me alone.
Each time when I need to hear those words,
Like sweet reminder I hear echoes once again.
"I AM"

Time is the passageway of hope.
Mysteries in life have reasons, some unknown.
We must never stop our inward search.
Listen carefully, silent echoes speak the truth.
"I AM"

Congratulate yourself for having echo.
Inner voice speaks to you whenever you're alone.
Train yourself to never be dismissed.
The source is not your ego but a power from within.
"I AM"

72

Moon Above My World

moon above my world
fish beneath my city
inside journey
my imagination with me

goodness in my heart
I am no saint when it comes to living
solitudes spent in purgatory
not every gesture willing
redefining morals
I climb church towers to see tomorrows

fantasy is where each mind escapes to
I keep my inner child near me
the only freedom I will ever have
in this world
is where I choose to be

when river empties
my fish begin to fly
my mind not always with me
in this
the world I make it

73

Would You Save Me If You Could?

Untold stories from times once lived,
selective memory my only savior.
Opinionated by not every story great,
reminiscing without acceptance of the past.
Anonymous with lessons learned.
Morality needs revising.
I would save you if I could.

Childhood memories getting stuck
in prickly bushes of raspberry dreams,
archiving places that would otherwise bring tears.
I keep places hidden where only I can find them,
bubble gum pressed beneath classroom desk.
I call upon my mirror to save me.
Compassion disappearing. Reasons getting lost.
Would you save me if you could?

I see politics being played
without respect for human rights,
nepotism racing forward, serving fools without disgrace,
politicians escaping duties, promises always pending,
citizens losing voice, dignity of mankind dying.
One person sees this world in need of rescue.
Would you save me if you could?

74

Another Stone Has Stayed
(Camino de Santiago)

I returned a second time to get acquainted
with my inner self.
The first time I went I awakened all my senses
where inner child had been forgotten, where smiles
had become fatigued.

It took many miles to find myself,
to have a deeper sense of who I am.
This journey started as a child.
I am energy, I am freedom, I am love.
When I am crying, I am more than simple tears.

I keep returning to same place within my heart,
to better understand who others are to me,
without material, my possession.
I am energy, I am freedom, I am love.
When I am crying, I am more than simple tears.

I go well beyond tomorrows, everyday acquainting,
blisters of heart no longer hurting.
A thousand bruises, each one a different reason why.
Each time I leave behind a little of myself,
each time returning home a different man.

Another stone has stayed,
all my problems now best friends.
All my joys define me. The Camino stays
within my heart.
I pray forever lasting.

75

Ballet Butterfly
(her passion dies)

Born to a butterfly, I was learned new thoughts.
Escapist to a human crime, I changed my face.
Dancing eyes to dancing shoes, my lady found a dancing mind.
Awakened from life's darker stage, I am the lady came a dancer.

And my dancer was a lady.
Puppet of grace, friending to the wind,
walking through the air,
flying over people's faces,
people's places weren't my own.

The audience sees a dancer.
With open eyes they do not know
my open eyes are blind.
Ovation faces (have the audience).
Watch me, and I'll fly.

One man with a moustache curled up high, grabs and
holds on tight. Another coughs relief. Another
shifts and winks his mate. My dancer
moves first rate.

The stage gets bigger. Lights
get brighter. The audience more entangled.
A tear falls from my dancer's eyes. A clap is heard.
Out of step, I am stopped.
(the dancer).

Thunder applauds before my flowers bloom.
Novice voices praise my encore feat.
I cut one stem to pass it on.
Blind eyes perceive my own defeat.

I bear for them my talent's best. One last step
without applause, I am the dancer,
I feel unmoved. Tears have gathered.
My emotions drowned. Where will I go?
(the dancer).

Rolling over bodies, I do not move.
Untangled from this human knot, with smile not my own,
a learned emotion now relieved of pain.
Dancing eyes to dancing shoes,
my passion succumbs a dancing death.

76

I Used My Flashlight

I used my flashlight
to get through late night woods.
In the morning I discovered
it's all about perspectives.

I saw winter horse harnessing neigh
upon finding spring.
I saw anatomy of a flower
being explicit over summer love.
When autumn arrived, I saw clouded sky.

It was sweet my journey.
I was awakened as many times
as I did dream.
The best was when my heart found me.

Now I reminisce on cotton clouds
atop heaven's lustful breeze.
I keep busy building rainbows
preventing raindrops from becoming storms.

Deep inside soul, my sanctuary.
I shall never again let dark return.
In gratitude,
you can hold my hand

77

Never Miss The Time It Takes

Train yourself
to never miss the time it takes.
Every moment has a beginning and an end.
Velocity of time may run too fast.
Avoid speeding pulse, slow it down.
Live every moment that you can.

Never miss the time it takes
to live your journey.
You are creator,
all mysteries here on earth your only.
Every moment becomes once lived,
each defining who you are.
You have evolved this far inside your name.
No other person can do the same.

Never miss the time it takes
to live your eyes.
Everything you see is colored by perspectives.
Every color
is what you through journey
have created.
Every day is dying,
another journey in the making.

Never miss the time it takes
to live your mouth.
Everything you say is archived for a lifetime.
Every word you speak
alters perspectives from anyone who listens.

What you say
becomes the image
everyone will remember always.
One mouth is all you have.

Never miss the time it takes
to live your touch.
Hug me dear, I need to cuddle.
Every human craves for touching.
Touch everything you simply can
within lawful reason and respect.
Acquaint your senses
You will feel your world is changing.

Never miss the time it takes
to live your taste.
Big party on this earth
belongs to the connoisseur you are becoming.
You are sommelier
for this day-may-be-your-only.
Everything you taste
prepares diet for your making.

Never miss the time it takes
to live your thoughts.
Where they gather is
up to each of us as planner.
The story you are acting
is the story they are telling.
A kind and friendly mind
will provide you better space.

Another day is born,
becomes an isolated journey.
Every moment gives a little
to time without regress.
Every journey a lifetime in the making.
Never miss the time it takes
to be yourself.

78

A Kiss Stealing Whispers

The war was in my eyes.
Now my soul collects flowers
cultivating memories past.
A kiss stealing whispers
from stories before untold.

A sea inside a grain of salt,
hold it to the light and you will see
history of all battles told.
The way to my heart
through a door made of steal.
I am wiser despite
memories restrict me.

Soul once darkened
by overwhelming night.
Sunrise saved me
introducing brightness to my skies.
Through inward journey
I started changing face.
All things began to glow.

Heart no longer lost in painstaking feud.
Soul inspired.
All darkness now removed.
Sunshine miraculously warming over soul.
A kiss stealing whispers,
from stories before untold.

79

I Don't Need You To Love Me

Whatever happens is supposed to happen.
Ever so slightly we are different every day.
Kiss this moment, enrich yourself, you cannot keep it.
Moments passing can never be returned.

I don't need you to love me.
I don't need you to understand what went wrong.
You can bleed my heart. You can break it too.
Dismiss my love it's up to you, I'll be fine.

My love is something precious.
Integrity is engraved somewhere deeper than flesh of heart.
I'll keep my love inside where it abundantly wants to grow.
It entirely belongs to me. It is mine to give
and mine when to let it go.

I Am The Soul Beside Me
(Camino de Santiago)

Keeping journey in my mind,
I need an *albergue* soon where I can rest.
I am frail from all this walking.

Without warmth from someone's heart,
without a needed hug,
I know not the map where I must follow.

Around every next bend in life's beckoning way,
a pilgrim there beside me.
I have sunrise to admire.

Let me learn to enjoy the solitude of every season.
As rocky as this road may be
a blister will not stop me.

Attached since birth to inward journey,
I am my own best friend.
My fate needs no one else to cling to.

One million steps it took me
to reach the Cathedral of my dreams,
jubilance of journey never ending

In praise of heart's content,
going alone growing stronger.
I am the soul beside me.

81

Poetry The Poem

Poetry can be an escaping song
from a grieving soul within.
Poetry can be romance expressed through words of love.

Poetry may captivate a bleeding heart.
The truth it tells can leave you in dismay
or frustrate when thinking of a better verse to say.

Poetry is much more than gracious words.
It can be defiance eradicating a wrongful world.
Writers describe things as no one other does.

Have a pen beside you, words may only visit once.

Poetry can be emotional discharge
when a wound is left unhealed
or when cloud nine shines brighter than the last one.

Poetry can be an image of yourself inside a private space.
When reality slaps you in the face,
poetry can help you look the other way.

82

Candy Floss

(nothing wrong with masturbation)

Fantasy of imagination
revisiting absent dream.
All my urges never aging,
bliss uprooted, memories fading.

Flowers finding autumn in their bloom,
everyone a season, everyone a song.
Pleasures I can find,
each time I do, I pull real hard.

Candy floss at country fair,
innocence of childhood without a care.
Sweetness sticky on my face,
I start craving when I see her.

Youth each time I'm set on fire,
sweet pollen in my system.
I keep busy extracting goodness.
We can harvest when we're young.

Fall in love,
young man's captive dream.
I get helpless when my mind starts craving;
other ways when she is absent.

At any age
I let thoughts seduce me.
All my powers in my hand,
relief I find when she's not with me.

83

Popsicle love

I may once again enjoy a blizzard
now with evidence of winter gone.
New fling helps me heal my heart.
Rejuvenating it is to start again.
I am in love, this time for real,
and my woman craves banana.

Once she took me in the car.
I had never been that far.
New love does me good.
Those who left me did me wrong.
I am in love, this time for real,
and my woman craves banana.

I love my darling true again.
She melts my heart when she is near.
Bliss is how she makes me feel.
She knows what love is all about.
Life has never felt so good,
and my woman craves banana.

84

Dark Love Unlike Chocolate

Heartbroken was not the tranquility I was seeking.
Perpetually my woman was a season.
Each time inside a different storm, my love would say goodbye.
By love she was corruption.

Return she would soon after
to break my heart yet another time,
each time more fiercely than before.
By love she was disaster.

Killing me slowly,
in exchange for what her ego wanted.
Prudish heart, she never had a clue,
teeter-totter was her game.

I became her storm chaser
pursuing episodes of hurt.
Outside a place where vows are kept
she was a darling and a quirk.

Never could I predict
when things were about to change.
Suddenly and without due warning
my life became insane.

She became my princess and my castle.
I attached all hurt to her.
My iron lady had a crystal heart.
Cloud nine disappearing from her mind.

The heart is more than flesh they say.
Impossible it is to give half away.
Love for reasons of insanity,
each time her ways would break me.

She kept leaving me in times of dream.
Each time I kept awakening to her game.
Dark love unlike chocolate,
My heart became insane.

85

Sandcastles To Return To

I have had childhoods.
Some I remember.
Some I have blocked.
Each one has changed me.
Each one I have grown from.

I walked through storms
letting rains downpour upon me.
Altered through lifetimes,
on happier days
I built castles in the sand.

I will return God willing
to revisit innocence from my past,
to leave behind all those who did me harm.
My siblings all dismissed me.
I have no brothers.

Where now I am, I shall stay forever.
I have sandcastles to return to.
If some of them should tumble
I promise to rebuild them.

Spiritual Sounds Of The Camino
(Camino de Santiago)

With timeless courage
I close my eyes
to let tranquil mind be accompanied
by orchestra of sound
every Pilgrim with me

Camino joy
an element of mind
marveling inside journey
every voice transparent
solitude each day altered
'Buen Camino' calling

Inner child returns to surface
innocence of expression
favorable to unconscious spirit
swept away
by beckoning journey
church bells telling time

Sister Maria's voice
a shadow of my soul
passageway to inner being
cathedral chants I have inside me
joyously permitting heart to cry

Sunrise awakening Pilgrim voice
each *Albergue* touching smiles
little miracles meandering
every moment spiritual

yellow arrows guiding

Crosses marking sanctuary
where some souls have stayed
I bless myself to keep them safe
with loving spirit in my prayer
heaven stays beside me

Spiritual sounds of the Camino
500 miles instrumental to my soul

87

Like A Rainbow Never Knowing Storm

A tree falling in a forest
with no one there to hear it,
I kept telling her
I love you.

Her problem went much deeper.
My energy produced no echo.
My words she would not hear.

On mountain edge she pushed me.
I did not fall. Love saved me.
Now I sing with angels.
Eternity, never letting go.

Without love becomes a struggle,
like an ocean without waters,
like a rainbow
never knowing storm.

Before returning home,
no soul can be so poor,
to find there is no heaven
on earth before one dies.

Darling
hear me when I say these words
another time,
I love you.

88

To Where Once We Were

Flowers in your garden look so real.
In your world very few things do.
You are in my heart to stay.
True love cannot be buried.
Could anything return you
to where once we were?

Full moon tranquil in my sky,
let memories return untroubled
to stay calm within our waters.
Moon shadow never leaving.
Could anything return you
to where once we were?

After storm I stay waiting for your rainbow.
In darkened skies you have no shadow,
no interval before your thunder.
Without you, every day becomes forever.
Could anything return you
to where once we were?

One crucifix is all my journey has.
My rose has only bud.
In solitude I keep on waiting,
my soul forever seeking.
Could anything return you
to where once we were?

89

Inside Oceans

Sometimes I break into tears.
Sentiments start running wild.
Being too sensitive feels out of place,
my feelings start running profoundly deep.
Beautiful things get soaking wet.
I have oceans. I have rivers. I have dreams.

I cry for very little reason.
Floodgates of pain wash everything afloat.
First I drench things with a smile,
then I cannot hold things in.
Beautiful things escape as tears.
I have oceans. I have rivers. I have dreams.

Finally I build a dam instead
to hold emotions deep inside.
I cannot easily express them out.
In deeper waters I cannot swim.
Now drowning seems to be my fate,
inside oceans, inside rivers, inside dreams.

90

Flash Mob Hugging

hug a stranger back
this will change the world
five people more not less
go armed with TLC
to an open public place
to ambush innocent bystanders
with friendly interruptions
to collecting hugs
involving people from all walks of life
to collecting hugs for free
crossing bridges between races and religions
to collecting hugs for you and me

excuse me please can we share a hug
this hug's for you
you must share it too
spreading awareness
celebrating we are engaged in peace
happy to share this hug with you
as Canadians we are inclusive
no one needs to be a stranger
everyone is now related
making love
through friendly hugs
flash mob hugging
creating smiles

91

Terracotta Soldier

In farmer's field looking down upon the ground
I could see 8000 soldiers looking upwards to the sky.
I am far from them. History helps me understand,
they are nearer than they seem.

520 horses galloping inside my vision, history
clearly with me. Everything appears as it did back then,
few years the only difference.

Terracotta soldier you have some flaws. You've lost
your head, your eye sight gone. With bonding power
you can be my force but first you must accept me as I am.

Deep beneath a ton of soil, first emperor put you inside clay.
Armor shattered beyond belief, rebuilding I will help you.

History buried in timeless toil, purgatory not a place to stay.
Challenges were put there not to stop you.
On the other side, all problems solved.

From another farmer's field, I see broken hands toiling hard.
An army beneath their ground protecting,
furthest from the truth it seems.

92

Sparkles In My Eyes

I want to share my sparkles,
lips this close.
You can be there always
in my glory, in my bliss.

We can cross this bridge together,
go all the way to heaven.
First get inside my hug.
Darling be there with me.

There's a pulse inside my heart
each time I hold you in my arms
it makes me want to love you.
Darling be there with me.

Don't get off until the music stops.
My heart is in your song.
For you, I am forever.
Darling be there 'til the end.

93

At Ripened Age

At ripened age before winter greets me
I know I should have changed my ways.
Too many times life proved me wrong.
Second chances come too late.

The loves that left me, hearts did depart.
Intriguing are the stories each one told.
They are all kept caged inside my heart;
I have only memories left to hold.

At ripened age my journey took me far.
Now crowned with thorns, rose petals fallen.
Through broken hearted seasons, I made my way.
Hearts not followed, left roads untaken.

Passageways sometimes led me astray,
Inside my soul, everlasting hand to hold.
Overcoming sadness, seemingly no place left to go.
At ripened age, I have come this far.

94

I Will Love Her with My Body

Photos I took are mine.
Memories belong to me.
From afar she says I cannot keep them.

Beyond oceans of turbulence,
way past where closure first began,
as long as my heart bleeds profusely
she keeps dismissal within her reach.

I will hold my love
tightly in forgiving arms.
When she denies my heart
I will love her with my body.

From her lady glass
I will drink champagne,
marinade my grapes,
I pray she lets me.

Until perceived lies are drunk,
I will keep happiness close at heart.
Love's demise is not invited.
Another hour of same will calm her.

95

In Winter Standing

I found some old pages
taken directly from my youth.
Everything happens for a reason.

I am that person.

Tears humbled me every step along my way.
Life robbed visions I had of spring.
Journey down poured on my summer.

I am that person.

My ego became weathered.
Seasons never did return.
New hope became harder to remember.

I even lost September.

Journey gave me lifetime, not the calm I had desired.
My friends all went before me,
leaving me, the only man in winter standing.

I am that person.

96

Magnificent Failure
(Bipolar Energy)

another final storm
love's total devastation
monstrous anger devouring innocent dream
harsh words spoken with unprecedented rage
magnificent failure
destructive
bipolar energy

dialogue never returning home unwounded
fresh wounds bleeding from innocent side of hurt
each encounter on slippery edge of another closure
composure self-destructing inside friendly fire

ego thrives on someone never being wrong
never at fault yet storms they keep surprising
one never knows what is kept inside hidden cage
demeanor is uninvited

love becomes the unwanted song
devastation not intended
I know all lines before rehearsal
everything calm before monster starts escaping
magnificent failure
destructive
bipolar energy

97

Age Of White
(Inside REMIC Rapids Park)

Inside REMIC Rapids Park
along the Ottawa river
I prepared a barbecue
and a serving of secondary motive.

Forbidden to drink alcohol inside city parks,
we drank wine concealed in plastic glasses.
Rules are broken
only when juveniles get caught.

Seniors never look conspicuous.
Lunch without wine
uninspiringly
English,
discouraged in Ottawa by Federal Law.

I was tickled
for having chance to use
my notwithstanding clause.

As seniors we learn to improvise.
Grandfathered from being politically correct,
rebellious just the same;
as Canadians,
I'm sorry, neither of us were willing.

Another glass of wine.
Lips were being planted.
Second age was coming.

Life is built on seasons changing.
Burning with desire she was primed.
I gave her one more glass on time.

For dessert I brought a hammock.
I hung it over water's edge
between two trees
out of sight
from where stone people
keep standing in the river,
close enough
to where summer breeze
rejuvenates
the age of white.

As seniors
we claimed diplomatic immunity.
We could turn any moment
into an independent country.

Grandma's panties came off like melted butter.
Her bra hung over hammock's edge.
Without a cloud of hesitation,
we got busy before things had time to wrinkle.

I felt river breeze on everything she was touching.
I could hear the sound of river moaning.
Grannies affection cried ripples in my eyes.

A few meters away
there were people passing by.
They never knew
how close they were
to my perspective.

I was within arm's length agreement,
standing on my own,
intensely focused
on a subject more inspiring.

Inside a place where
bliss begs to stay,
unless someone cut my rope
I was well fastened to the moment.

Making love in a hammock
during daylight hours
is as heavenly as it gets.
Crème brûlée would not have tasted any better.

Grandma, she saw stars.
I heard music playing.
Angels above us watching,
everything else heavenly and divine.
I could come again, granny's smile whispered.

98

Bridge Over Bipolar Waters
(Restated)

Let us embrace
one another and in defiance
of what we are told
we can or cannot do, let us drink
wine from the same wine goblet
to honor our differences
in the name of peace. I do not know
what is written above. I need not know
where you are coming from
nor must you know
where I have been. The future is about finding
common ground so we may stand united.

We are brothers and sisters. We are fathers
and sons. We are mothers and daughters.
We are flesh first before religion. We are hearts
and souls sharing one same universe.
May your God bless my sons and daughters
and may my God bless your sons and daughters
equally. There is one universe
where we must all coexist. We are
of the same family belonging to
one global community.
The country worth saving is called...
Peace on Earth.

99

Removing Water From Your Ego

I am no longer where you want me.
Inside my castle,
I hurt less this time on purpose.

Undoing pain,
removing water from your ego.
I am not insane.
Your perspectives still need changing.

Bring nothing forward from the past.
Everyone should explore second nature
before changing mind for better score.

Happy memories are worth
ten times their weight in gold.
Let's remember to forget excruciating pain.
Let's hurry up, not everything lasts forever.

100

On Untold Edge

I did not go seeking darkness.
Darkness found me just the same.
She played me as an escape route.
Cheating housewife was her game.
Down on her knees to make new friends;
sinfully, my innocence was devoured.

Insecurity clinging to untold edge,
thriving on lies,
anxiously relocating.
Nikita lives in a world she calls her own.
Self-proclaimed in the art of Zen,
each day a different person.

Wiping friendships clean,
other voids become her victims.
Troubled ego
meticulously keeping score,
tweeting victories to her friends
blatantly removing mystery.

preying on unpretentious men,
un-liked by lover's dream,
once gone never missed.
Every day she is a season changing
preaching Zen to anyone who listens,
forever burning new built bridges.

On untold edge of circular vision,
what goes around finds passageway in.
Seeking harvest, romance in disguise
counting cocks, every kiss inside a lie.
She lets heartless in through empty soul
everyone passing through one same door.

101

Third Time In Heaven
(Camino de Santiago)

Third time in heaven,
this time I cannot say goodbye.
A few more steps will guide me.
Yellow Arrows will help me find them.

Pilgrim love
adding purity to my prayer.
People busy sharing journey
where some have stayed with crosses.

Life's blister healing in my heart,
all good souls embrace me.
I return each time to find myself,
Hail Mary when I get there.

Camino miracles, truth awakening,
heaven-on-earth my blessing.
Through journey, nature as my witness,
Hail Mary when I get there.

102

Retrieving Heart

Failures darken my pathway forward.
Treasures I seek may not be there.
I gave her my entire heart.
She took from me my only pleasure.

Retrieving heart is not an easy task.
Some pieces stay forever broken.
Journey back, one more pain to carry.
Re-awakening, who am I becoming?

My inner child perpetually ready to surrender,
Walk on ice; never let your heart deepen in the sand.
My wisdom keeps persuading. Stay near dear child,
We will make it to the end together.

103

Moments With Amore

In *Rome* I went no further.
I may never get there.
My dream was to go to *Venice*.

I would rather swim in *Venice* waters
than let a dream escape the prospect of a kiss.
On a gondola exchanging kisses, *that's amore*
now lost to lover's quarrel.

Heart's villain stealing coins from *Trevi* fountain,
every wish, a treasure pending.
My coin denied under rage of hopeless passage.
Reverberating echo, unwanted by lover's song.

I tried *rose rosse*,
in her waters they quickly wilted.
I tried *vino dolce*,
sweet tasting like delicious kiss.

Waters evaporate in *Venice*
each time I remember my *signora* saying *Ciao*.
Under full moon, lips denied.
Rage more passionate than lover's kiss.

I would not hear my song in *Venice*.
Love kept its dignity, this time never leaving *Rome*.
I found my *bella* at a sidewalk Caffè *in Via Veneto*.
I kissed the lady, she kissed *Amore*.

104

Rainbows Now In Braille

From the other side of smile
I can feel jubilance I once knew.
Now vanished behind fierce storm,
my sunshine taken with it.

All of me consumed.
Only memories now remain.
Let each one go, I must.

Without seeing my tomorrow
darkness inspires little hope.
True love dismissed
by unprecedented fate
leaves me without clear vision.

I can cuddle with my past.
One kiss remaining.
I will share it with my soul.

I find lost clouds inside darkest prayer.
Through inward journey
I see myself as blinded.

Hope is reborn before patience lost.
Rainbows now in braille.
My heart becomes new sight.

105

Heart In Free Fall

heart in free fall
eyes in can't believe
on cloud nine she left me
every dream forever gone
sentiments falling fast
turbulence never letting go
I pray I get upon her kiss
sky too high to fall
parachute me to the ground
don't leave me 'till I'm on my feet
please wait until I'm down

106

I'll Let My Echo Stay

I can hear you from afar
when winds are in your favor.
You can hear me too
if you listen to my echo.

Two dozen roses once made you cry.
When you left, you shed no tears.
Before sweet memory leaves you,
I'll let my echo stay.

Lover's quarrel, all my seasons absent.
Lover's quarrel, distant winds are not my savior.

Inside purgatory awaiting spring?
This cage has no more bars.
It's my heart that keeps me.

Heart as savior.
I'll let my echo stay.
I'll let my echo stay.

107

Second Heart

Each time my darling leaves me,
my heart gets in a wilt and dies.
From scattered halves I reconstruct
valid reasons to survive.

She did not come to watch me die
when first heart was broke in half.
Closure had come this near.

When love awakened,
a second heart was waiting,
a second life I then possessed,
a second soul was mine.

Despite all omens she keeps on giving
misery I do not need.
Each time I hurt when she is with me,
Much worse when she dismisses.

108

Spent Memories

When love is gone
you can have it always
in memory, nothing more.

To cross heart's bridge
after love is burnt,
in spent memories love will stay.

Golden each one remains
preserving smiles past.
Every last kiss, once tried now gone.

Let love depart
all treasures lost.
Have no more mind for waiting.

109

Dragonfly In Spain
(Camino de Santiago)

Memories staying deep within,
I wear them as a sweater around my heart
woven in the fabric of everlasting love.

Upon entering *Santa Catalana de Somoza*,
my Camino feet well worn, my *mochila*
at its heaviest of the day.

Darkest clouds had built a fortress in the sky
when beneath forgiving rainbow,
I found a pathway to my soul.

I prayed this day would never end.
With perseverance I kept on going,
never wishing for what could not be.

Safe passageway to a spiritual world within;
all my soul was with me, including
before my eyes, the illusion of a dragonfly.

110

Arctic Bouquet

arctic flower
I find you when I least expect you
my soul sees all your native colors
warmth of imagination each one tells
eyes feel wiser for having seen you

left unpicked
you will be there again tomorrow
if only love could be so true
arctic flower you have no thorns
I will change my ways to know you

innocence of unprotected nature
embracing devastating winds
accepting frost the way it is
sunshine strong
you wear upon your wisdom
all in spirits good
nature accepts you as its friend

wild flowers gracing innocence of heart
colors softly sweeten the pathway I must follow
arctic bouquet
your treasures I have seen adorn me
together we will sing
all things good with nature
my love for you much wiser

111

One Of Me Is Broken
(Second Version)

I spend my journey collecting treasures. I keep them
secure inside my heart. All of them I miss profoundly
never with possession.

My inner child is destined never to get old. Things I say
with simple words start aging only when you listen.

I see myself in childhood, one of them is hungry.
Half my plate is empty. I share without a question.
Alone each day I am, my rejuvenating self.

One of me is broken. I search inside to fix it.
Perspectives forever changing, light stays
everlasting in my soul never losing spirit.

Love defines me. Everything I see tells me who I am.
To you, I am a reflection of your psyche.
Things you see belong to you.

I live each day inside my journey
profoundly never with possession.

112

Tears Become My Blood

Everything I ever wanted.
I saw her one last time.
Now every wound re-opened.

Tears become my blood.
Let's abandon all life's worries.
Let's revisit all that matters.

Love
With tears of joy I wrote this note. I have good reasons why. Words once spoken cannot be changed. Let's bury all our devils. Love can last forever.

The bridge she did not burn
Took her home to where she never left.
Permanence is what she feared the most.
Now two hearts stay forever hurting.

Everything she ever wanted.
She saw me once last time.
Now every wound re-opened.

113

My Heart Is In Her Storm

Her ocean is restless.
My heart is in her storm.
No more stars above her castle.
No more words inside my song.

I wear no shoes, no sandals.
I walk on the edge of hope.
My savior comes tomorrow.
Today all dreams are gone.

I would go alone
but she walks beside me.
In my mind I cannot leave her.
Without destiny, I would have no soul.

114

Abandoned Memory

wilted flowers in my mind
thorns inside bleeding heart
a fragment of abandoned memory
too painful for my conscience
too wretched for my calm
returned uninvited
to a deeper sense of inner being
each time
I hurt again

I put all dark behind me
evergreens inside forest mist
I create the illusion of a dream
a place where I can go and hide
a place where things are vaguely seen
unwanted hurt
each time when dark returns
I fabricate an imaginary world
within my pain

as far away from bleeding heart
as far away as life will let me

115

A Million Steps Has Left A Saint
(Camino de Santiago)

My soul
now feels a mile high.
I feel as strong as
last mountain climbed.
I never lose one cloud from nine.
My heart stays with me.

Willingly I accept
best moments disappearing from my sight.
Within each step
I keep yellow arrows in my vision.
Spirit inside defines me.

It takes me days to go an hour.
Blisters slow me even further.
Journey alters life forever.
Perspectives changing deep within,

The cathedral,
I bring it home inside my heart.
Every other treasure,
I learned to let each one go.
A million steps has left a saint
inside my soul, to carry on.

116

Spring Blossoms

The beauty of Spring fever,
I have blossoms when I see her.
She is always there
telling me how much she loves me.
When I awaken from my dream
I have only strength to call her name.
The keeper of my heart, she never listens.

Somewhere deep within
Spring blossoms never bloom.
Warm blooded, cloudy sky
I have feelings when I cry.
Spring keeps leaving, becomes my fate.
Beneath frozen waters of my soul
there is another winter waiting.

As I grow older
Spring gets colder,
Spring blossoms forever aging.
With wrinkled love I reminisce,
memories begging to survive.
The keeper of my heart,
she never listens.

117

Darling We Have Baggage

Everything sounds absurd when taken out of context.
You never stop accusing, insinuations never ending.
All that you say is true from your perspective.
Darling you have baggage.

With darkest cloud removed, you are my guiding star.
You are the echo of everything I say.
Times we seldom spend together provide moments of escape.
Darling you have baggage.

Absence of your heart provides unruly celebration.
Your ego is entangled. I've said this from the start.
Energy forces need aligning. Your tone needs starting over.
Darling you have baggage.

Ask me anything when our hearts are back together.
Do not ask me from afar when egos are dismissing.
Let's free our minds beyond where past has always kept us.
Darling you have baggage.

Do not feel resentment. You are in a world you never left.
Staying where you are, you were never where you stayed.
Carrying grievances is misgiving.
Darling we have baggage.

118

All Signs Say She's A Keeper

I think my hammock
will fit perfectly,
her and I together.
Once we tie the knot,
I am staying there forever.
The comfort of her soul so sweet,
all signs say she's a keeper.

I think her lips
will provide sanctuary
for eternal kiss.
The songs she sings
will mesmerize my heart.
Love has found me.
All signs say she's a keeper.

I think in bliss
every love song sounds the same.
Every time undoing lonely in my mind,
last time too,
bells were ringing in my head.
Love is but a sacred place.
yet each time when we're apart,

all my love gets flimsy.

119

I Chased Her One Last Time

I sought armistice.
It came with shame.
Satisfaction has a price.
She wanted war.
In denial,
I chased her one last time.

Our minds on slippery edge,
surrender neither of us would.
My heart keeps seeking another reason,
I think I may have lost one.
Love learns late when memories cling.
I chased her one last time.

Her name engraved inside stubborn heart.
Remove this stone, I know not how.
Storms all vanish over time.
I pray one more season could be mine.
She has nothing more to offer.
I chased her one last time.

120

I Bled With A Heart That Would Not Die

In this world, unorthodox to who I am,
I am a rebel first. Spending two years on a crucifix
I bled with a heart that would not die.

I accepted circumstances, believing the only solution
was to live with pain. In the middle of winter is when
I need spring flowers most. Being separated was hardest
on me. I know this because I could feel my pain.

A calloused heart is damaging to the mind, sense
of perception altered. Each time my love would leave
for soul, a season lost is all I kept.

A madman lives with hope; never does he know,
illusion is his friend. Love becomes a much
needed medicine. There is no escaping symptoms.
Happiness gets traded for addiction
or helplessly stranded between purgatory
and never knowing when.

From opposite sides of earth, distant storms kept
preventing closure. I could not count the number of times
closure is all she wanted, nor could I count the number
of times she expressed willingness to start again.

Purgatory needs a better plan. Where we keep our treasures
is up to each of us. At any age, time can reawaken.
Oceans divide. Help me find a pathway through this storm.
Bless my heart. Lead me to your garden.

121

She Stole My Only Copy

she stole my only copy
lust momentarily stole my soul
desire throbbed its way inside her
my soldier standing was succumbed

insight into where I want to be
all my fantasies because of her came true
soaking wet with fifteen year old smile
guilt could not have tasted better

passions engaging
she pulled my trembling ego closer
engraving her name inside bragging rights
with devilish force I let her
waters enflamed with fire
she took my boyhood with her

breaking innocence
selfishly with intent
I was but one more count for her
she claimed my jewels
I touched her treasure
then grateful to the villain for her theft
I let her go
my stage was set

122

She Keeps Burning All Her Treasures

She keeps burning all her treasures. Her secrets
she will not share. Zen master, every day unbiased.

Her world is full of burning bridges. She keeps seeking love
on other people's shores. A master of illusion,
frivolously in pursuit of Zen.

She was glowing on the night of the harvest moon.
Naked beauty spread beneath stars of darkened skies,
intensely focused, every kiss a passing season.

Her heart each time before it dies faithfully returns to Zen
setting everything ablaze to quench life's disappearing passion.
Deception is her charm, exploiting tired vows of marriage.

Traces of sin I left inside her cheating grace. Righteous it is
to let something go when it has no intrinsic value.
Easy to let heart be victim when bliss awakens sooner.

She keeps burning all her treasures. Her secrets she will not share.
Zen master is her trade. She knows it very well.

123

Before Nature Gave Me Feelings

My eyes landed frozen on the shore-line
of ego's guilty cleavage.
Little brother caged behind metal zipper
feeling imprisoned
quivering to get released.

Without eyes, he knew what I had seen.
I have morals too. It is not her heart I seek.
Claiming victory is much the only thing I need.
Instinct will show me what I need to know.
Once surrendered, I shall let the lady go.

Passion emptying into ocean,
all my river flowing.
Moments riddle through my mind.
I may get back from pleasure.
I worry my soul may never follow.

It's not for me to judge the way I am.
She embraced me tightly as if I wanted more.
Glitter in her eyes identifying this as love.
I found a tear above her lip and left it there to dry.
As quickly as I could, I left her,

before nature gave me feelings.

124

When Peace Returns From War

Peace is won
not by lottery nor by prayer.
Against totalitarian dictatorship
is never found by waiting, never
when in despair.

Do souls exist when hearts get lost?
When does peace return from war?

Too many people hiding behind their faces
God understands when man must kill.
All good souls forgotten.

Those coming home, many wounded in their minds.
Their hearts have been where morals cannot go,
spiritual codes buried somewhere lost.

In this world where you and I must live:
Churches are divisive. Morality is in decay. Politicians
are bought and sold. Votes matter more than
human rights. Governments cheating, Sense of ethics,
everyone devalued. Values lost to crime.

Rub yourself a little faster or get a masseuse
to do it for you. This world is doomed.
You could have saved it if you tried.
You could have saved it
if you tried.

125

Eight Minutes Of Descent

My soul escapes into mystical sky.
Shattered heart buried on mountain top.
Fear overcome by last moments of surrender,
breathing last scream.
Eight minutes of descent.

Illusions I hold inside, disappearing fast.
Inner being journey takes me further and beyond.
It's too late to kiss you.
Tomorrow's embrace no longer having pulse.
Eight minutes of descent is not enough.

I gave you garden's best.
You gave me harvest I desired.
Heart's content once exceeded all my sorrows,
I wish I had tomorrow.
Eight minutes of descent is all I have.

A lifetime vanishing inside darkened flight.
Why am I being called away?
My soul now distant from my flesh,
surrendering to let another season pass.
Eight minutes of descent.

126

Inward Child Of My Pain

cynicism of journey
camouflaged as innocence
built its storm inside my shelter
every kiss once loved
now poison

banquet to most painful thorn
memories inspired by never letting go
I scratch on wound
and hurt keeps bleeding

she is the inward child of my pain
drenched in hurt inside me crying
repeatedly
letting heart be bled

I have nowhere else to go but inward
sheltered by a deeper storm within
my darkest cloud
keeps raining

brilliant ego never letting go
some pains will stay forever
closure
my only savior

Let Love's Bridge To Drama Fall

another time she is mine
another time she leaves me
my heart in waters
deeper than my soul
pain, I miss you
tears, come home
inside broken romance
I have no more hurt to bleed

you showed me
vigorously both sides of storm
forever in my heart you stay
pain, I miss you
tears, come home
you keep returning
repeatedly each time
to say good-bye

let love's bridge to drama fall
next time you cross it
on my side to stay
pain, I miss you
tears, come home
desire in my garden
harvest grows
love not forgotten

128

Broken Promise

Temper is your bee bite.
I am your chase away.
Can you taste the salts
of failure in my tears?
Can you see the pain
that I am feeling?
Can you look beyond
where there is no tomorrow?

You see me
as the cause of all your anger.
I see you as a storm
that never ends.
Can you feel me in your silence
when I am nowhere there beside you?
Can you hold my hand
when I need you from afar?
Can you cry my tears?
Can you feel the slightest of my pain?

I am but a broken heart to you.
To me you are a broken promise.
Tell me, where can we embrace
inside moments that have no future,
inside moments that have no past?
I'll meet you there.

I become unsettled
by every day another question.
I should not have waited for the answers.
Can you armistice with me
when we cannot find peace through fighting?

Can you let happiness flow through your veins
to reciprocate a smile?
Can you chase away your anger?
Can you be with me ...one last time?

Poison in your ego
applauds the grand finale of our romance.
I'll hug you just as strong.
I am your other half.
Can you hurt unselfishly
to relieve my pain?
Can you smile
when wishing me pleasure and forgiveness?
Can you bury unwanted past
and admit our love was real?

129

Zen Love

We keep wetting every adjective with penetrating thoughts.
I am curious to see how deep this journey takes us.
Crossing boundaries where tease caresses bliss,
this is a novel journey without a promise land.
Blessings in desire,
energies hurriedly merging. We should.

Passionate foreplay interacting with timeliness of journey,
heart-pounding appetites shared with gestures in disguise.
Our ice is broken, now over the bridge to another shore.
Every trickle, every taste, sinfully sweet, deliciously seeking
I am ready to devour
wherever your nectar flows. We should.

Despite we each have raging fires,
you and I have burning hearts.
Lips glued together, eyes breathing fire,
hands touching lava, it doesn't matter if you're a liar.
Penetrating bliss, watering flames of Zen desire,
blind heartedly getting wet
ferociously for awhile. We should.

I'll keep my gems inside
until my passion dies.
Tomorrow I will not know you.

130

Inside My Soul, Emotions Save Me

mysteries abound
energies surround me
sometimes colliding with who I am
thank god I still have dreams
stars still twinkle in my sky
the moon above
shines so bright
thank god
life's journey
keeps most things right

my universe awakens
each time with sparkles in my eyes
inside my soul, emotions save me
thank god I made my way
to a place inside your heart
everything I feel is real
love is all I need
peace on earth, another matter
for now
I'll stay here for a while

131

Masturbation
(Insane Lover For A Day)

Spring fever each day returns,
same winter never willing.
I can be my foresight.
I can be your ego screaming.
Thoughts connecting through heart alive
in archives burning fire,
without which my system would implode.
Insane lover for a day.

Lonely spirit each day succumbs
beyond boundaries sometimes going.
Oceans I have prayed.
Lust brings joy to awaiting bliss
with every thrust, a happy smile.
Inner psyche receiving hugs,
central station, no one there.
Insane lover for a day.

Imagination upside down,
dancing mind has gone astray.
Toying thoughts start prompting pleasure,
heated lady in desire,
river in it, water flowing.
Inside solitude, every pleasure shared.
Silk umbrella never needed.
Insane lover for a day.

132

Silence Too Loud

We met without planning.
I took that as cue for
everlasting. All her beauty came with baggage.
Love's doom deviously got in my way. Her anger
started raging. My woman became
uncontrollably loud.

Carefully I learned to choose my words.
There was nothing I could do to calm her.
She started dwelling
in a distant state of mind.

Perpetual solitude
corrupted all my senses.
I discovered by changing one word
I could alter mood.
I touched her where age permitted.
Cleverly I relieved her storm. Overcast
started clearing.

No more outbreaks, no more raging anger.
For better or for worse, she changed her ways.

Then she started analyzing
everything she imagined I was thinking
until silence became too loud, dismissals even louder.

Quietly she dispersed every season from my soul.
If my heart should ever let her go,
I will build another journey.

133

Man Gets Old

Apples wrinkle when left un-harvested.
Apathy accepts a shriveled heart.
Man gets old when bliss no longer matters.

Turbulence of unresolved storm pacifies clouded eyes.
Rainbows disappear beyond horizon of spirit dying.
Let your soul have window. Let your heart have bridge.

Footprints vanish in the sand. Soon time will have no shadow.
Never regret the road once travelled. It stays not far behind you.
Let your soul have window. Let your heart have bridge.

Old man, don't surrender. Take time to sing another song.
Choose one with lyrics that last forever.
Mother Nature will embrace you

in her arms to stay
and blanket you
through seasons yet to come.

134

Passageway To Autumn Soul

I know where heaven is.
September winds caressing,
my heart feels gently warmer.

Being born again my greatest pleasure,
each time she holds me,
each time when I am with her.

Before winter comes I want much more.
Divine I feel
in bliss of summer ending.

Heaven knows me by my name.
Forever in this season
please let me stay here longer.

135

Beneath Stars Awaiting

Never trust things you think are real
without first knowing who you are.
Everything is seen beneath clouded sky.
The universe decides from which perspective.

As great as love can be, it will one day measure
a few small grains of sand, you and I, then equal.

Flesh, as sanctuary.
Mind, an energy force within.
It's not too late to search for soul
before mind has left one's body.

Within each being, light has good intention
returns us to where destiny first intended.

Energy forces will without warning find
a resting place at journey's end.
A bridge will take us to another shore
where love will reawaken.

136

You Became My Flag

You became my flag, my country,
each day my national anthem.
Your songs were many.
Happily there were mornings after.

You became my planet,
the only universe where I could live.
Never needing to rehearse, I was yours forever.
Love thrives on freedom to survive.

Love keeps growing when hearts are free.
Then you started demanding I change for you,
to never letting me be myself.
Love since then has gone astray.

I tolerate this world faithful to my soul.
Unfitted to your world, I grow outside.
My love for you will never change.
Yet all my freedoms, I will live without you.

131

Demeanor

The secret forest
is heaven here on earth
where mindfulness befriends contentment
failing which
returns to reality.
She kept returning me.

The tranquil sound of silence
and the noise it sometimes makes
once inside heart,
the way out is hard to find.

Happy to be alive
or died and gone to heaven.
She awakened all my senses,
both sides of earth now hurting.

Thunder made me know her better.
Best are words when softly spoken.
Another bridge to nowhere burned.
This river nowhere going.

I advocate against all things that hurt.
Reconciliation is nowhere to be found.
I know myself the best I can.
Her demeanor I know much better.

I chased my past
reminiscing inside troubled mind.
Through every window another light.

She never waited for a reason.
With unexplainable came impudence and rage.
Forever I now stay wishing
her demeanor will one day change.

I did not pray inside the Cathedral
but my tears were real.

138

Dhyana And Dark Chocolate
(Bipolar Syndrome)

Seeing through my eyes, I am the only one who does.
My way of understanding, no other person can.
I am unique as much as I am different.

My perspectives go anywhere I take them.
They have taken journey to develop.
Ever so slightly, we keep changing every day.

I can tell you what I saw
but you will never see the same.
Before she left, she was everlasting love.

Our spirits prudish when we met, we mistook for love.
Her intentions heavenly and divine, so were mine,
it was her temper swings that hung me.

She bled all romance with excruciating pain.
Breaking my heart became the only way she could.
Before she left, love's crucifix was stained.

Colors of forgiveness kept me waiting for resolve.
When she started showing symptoms,
all my colors started running.

dhyana and dark chocolate

She can be any petal on my daisy.
Unstable energies befriending hearts on fire,
fulfilling empty spaces,
not as institutions have decided.

Another event is all this moment is.
The scent of after-storm
drenches spirit in my soul.
I will remember her with desire.

Arms around me strong,
I am not a Buddhist but a man.
Until love returns next time with heart,
I will stay just where I am.

139

Halfway Point Between Two Consenting Adults

Ladies who lunch
she was one of those,
I had that feeling.
She seduced me
using two chocolates and
some deliciously sweetened words.

As author of erotica,
she played me with everything she could.
If our smiles were to touch again,
I would need to be
more intuitive with my pen.

I was into her
imagining myself
as one of her up and coming characters.
I made it to first paragraph.

As laborer of a writing mind
I wanted to get inside
soft romance in her novel.
Her cleavage now endorsing
through an opening to her heart.
Lady of erotica, my mind was set on fire.

Before I even knew her name,
figuratively my heart was inside heaven.
Ice melts when thoughts escape.
I was at halfway point
between two consenting adults.

140

I Am Not Too Cold To Cuddle

Throughout winter mostly
despite living in frigid weather
I keep another layer.
Arms around me strong,
Canada goose inside my lining,
I am not too cold to cuddle.

Teach me how to dance.
French-kiss me first,
Champagne-love me with your smile.
I have tango in my heart,
refugees in my prayers,
sweet love indigenous to my soul.

Proud to be Canadian,
every color on my side,
every language in my sky.
Passport good anywhere I go,
you are welcome too,
inclusive with gay pride.

My icicles are slow to thaw.
Spring thru summer gone too fast.
Autumn season is a brilliant place to be.
Eskimo dream and you will see
I am not too cold to cuddle.

141

Spiritual Fracking
(Camino de Santiago)

Silence
is the sound of awakening soul
breathing sentiments of inner peace.
Inside quiet dream
I am alive;
my emotions reassure me.

Uphill I start
through clouded skies
of long awaited journey.
I let first village disappear
in hindsight where past shall stay.
(Saint Jean Pied de Port my starting point).

I find spiders along my way.
Spiders spinning ancient silk
unmoved by mountain's gentle breeze.
My prayers are clothed in hopeful dream.

In solitude
I become one with nature's toiling soul
windowing first rays of morning dew.
Tranquil thoughts embrace me.

In evolution to new beginning,
the universe
can be forgiving when it wants to.
Inside healing heart,
forgiveness is my savior.

I smile inward
seeking strength to reach the top
having energy to climb first mountain
before my shadow shortens.

I follow friendly Pilgrims way
of those who walked before me.
So much peace I have inside
and miles more to share.

Spiritual fracking
will clear the way to take me further.

Looking down from mountain top
I see a forest
beneath misty sky,
heaven-on-earth below me.

Put more dew beneath my eyes
my quiet tears will soon be dry.

In journey I have come this far
to reacquaint with inner child
before heaven tells me
all time has gone.

The last leap forward
is where paradise is found.
My tears stay wet.
I know they're real,
as real as when she left me.

Time wrinkles as I wait.
I hold her in my arms.
In greying memory
she is real again,
as real as mountain mist.

She set my mind on fire.
She put my soul at risk.
She altered time before she quit
leaving all hope inside me dying.

I am here this time
to walk beside
a shattered soul,
to set things straight
away from past,
in journey
to relinquish all my pain.

I gave my heart;
now take it back, this time I shall.

Over mountains I must go
carrying burdens,
happy to leave each one behind,
heavy stones no longer staying.

Heaven within each step now nearer,
Santiago knows,
in journey
deep sorrows cannot last.

142

She Is Less Than Half My Age

From mountain ledge
high above all wisdom,
life is witness
to much more than I can see.

I followed river's pulse
beyond where splash had first begun.
Ripples of inner bliss
stay inside me flowing strong.

When my imagination weakens,
when body ages faster than desire
comes the sorrow of hopeless dream,
smiles now lethargic.

She is less than half my age.
I am more than twice her wit.
She needs my autumn.
I need her spring.

Beneath autumn winds,
I am forced to follow instinct.
Time has ravaged all my guilt.
Life has taken all my sin.

143

Another Kiss Before I Die

Through fields and forests
where once we walked together,
I dreamt love stayed there waiting for us.

Should I go back to sleep to keep love real
or awaken early to watch love disappear?
Without you this novel has no ending.

I could never talk inside your kiss.
Between our lips many words would fail.
Please let me speak through dreams of heart.

My heart is real, it begs to stay.
Through seasons lost, each day I prayed.
My other half is gone, she left, you did.

I cannot fathom where this love is going.
I have pebbles weathered in my soul
each breath of journey forever hurting.

I await unchained, the man you knew.
I await in vain, for another kiss before I die.

Sweet memories nurturing
last chapter never ending

My Inner Child Crying

I have gone beyond the forest fire
Way past the storm at sea.
It's too late for my inner child crying.

When institutions told me war was in my eyes,
I came back each time safe
embracing knowledge seldom seen.

Wisdom brought me back from war.
In season late I finally learned
there was no time left on earth for me.

Before age accompanied me one last mile,
I walked where instinct warned me not to go.
Sanity on earth everywhere now sleeps.

Politics and religion are two big lies.
In praise of understanding last lesson learned,
I should have listened to my inner child crying.

Acknowledgements

Bhat Boy - Artist - Front Cover Artwork
Website: **www.BhatBoy.com**
Thank you Bhat Boy for your kindness and generosity
in providing artwork for the cover page.

Lois Siegel - Professional Photographer
Website: **www.siegelproductions.ca**
Thank you Lois for taking the best pictures ever.

Ingrid McCarthy – Author - Mentor
Website: **www.ingridmccarthy.com**
Thank you Ingrid for having patience galore.
I am forever grateful to you.

Caroline Frechette - Cover and Interior Book Design
Website: **www.carolinefrechette.com**
Thank you Caroline for your amazing talent.

Kevin T. Johns – Author - Writing Coach
Website: **www.kevintjohns.com**
Thank you Kevin, your enthusiasm is unmatched.

Facebook Community and Twitter Followers
Thank you to all Facebook friends and Twitter followers.
Much gratitude for frequent praise and encouragement received.

www.ingramcontent.com/pod-product-compliance
Lightning Source LLC
Chambersburg PA
CBHW032118090426
42743CB00007B/388